GUIDING S

GUIDING STARS

Four Guides for Christians on the Way

Stephen Oliver
Bishop of Stepney

First published in Great Britain in 2005

Society for Promoting Christian Knowledge
36 Causton Street
London SW1P 4ST

British Library Cataloguing-in-Publication Data
A catalogue record for this book is available from the British Library

ISBN 0–281–05731–1

1 3 5 7 9 10 8 6 4 2

Typeset by Graphicraft Ltd., Hong Kong
Printed in Great Britain by Ashford Colour Press

For Archdeacon Lyle, the Clergy and People
of Hackney, Islington and Tower Hamlets
in the Area of Stepney,
who are my teachers

Faith is to believe what you do not see;
the reward of faith is to see what you believe.

(Saint Augustine)

People go abroad to wonder at the heights of mountains,
at the huge waves of the sea, at the long courses of the rivers,
at the vast compass of the ocean, at the circular motion of the stars;
yet they pass by themselves without wondering.

(Saint Augustine)

Real knowledge, like everything else of value, is not obtained easily.
It must be worked for, studied for, thought for and, more than all,
it must be prayed for.

(Thomas Arnold)

Contents

Foreword   xi

Introduction   xv

Acknowledgements   xviii

Jesus' Summary of the Law   1

The Lord's Prayer   23

The Apostles' Creed   45

The Beatitudes   73

Foreword

At many points the gospel runs counter to much contemporary culture. Our culture has it that ulcers have become status symbols. There is little escape from competitive living and it seems as if the worst sin in our society is to have failed. Of course, it all takes its toll in eating disorders, anxiety or a fearful aggression.

What a tremendous relief it has been to many to discover that we don't need to prove ourselves to God. We don't have to do anything at all to be acceptable to God. That is what Jesus came to say, and for that he was killed. He came to say, 'Hey, you don't have to earn God's love. It is not a matter of human achievement. You are a child of divine love.'

The religious leaders of his day – bishops and presidents if you like – they couldn't buy that.

Jesus scandalized them. He ate with the riff-raff because he had come to seek and to find the lost.

He told the story of the Pharisee and the publican who went to pray. The Pharisee boasted that he was not like other men, especially that publican over there, whereas the publican hardly dared to lift his eyes to heaven. He knew his need, his unworthiness, and so he was acceptable to God and received God's gift because he was empty of self.

The Good News is that God loved me long before I could have done anything to deserve it. God is like the good shepherd who goes out looking for the lost sheep. A cuddly young lamb will hardly stray from its mother. It is the troublesome, obstreperous sheep which goes missing. It is this dirty, smelling, riotous creature who gets lost, and yet when it is found there is great rejoicing in heaven.

This is the gospel, and it is wonderfully life-affirming. Too often, religion is regarded as life-denying 'Don't do this and don't do the other', as a spoilsport wet blanket, stopping us doing the things we enjoy or letting us do them but with a guilty conscience. That is a travesty of the faith of Jesus Christ. Jesus lived life to the full. How else can we understand his concern to heal the sick and feed the

xi

hungry? He forgave sins to relieve God's children of unnecessary burdens. He rejoiced in the lilies of the field and the birds of the air. He is often depicted at dinner parties and weddings, where once he even supplied the wine when it had run out. In fact he was accused of being a bit of a drinker and a friend of sinners.

He declared by this open and welcoming attitude that all life, sacred and secular, material and spiritual, could not ultimately be divided because it all belonged to God, came from God and would return to God.

Again, too many religious people think a long serious face and holiness somehow go together. Yet Jesus was being funny when he pictured a man trying to find a speck in his brother's eye while a huge beam is sticking out of his own. You sometimes hear people say that the original sin committed by Adam and Eve was related to sex. If it was, then it certainly wasn't very original! What nonsense. When God said they should be fruitful and multiply, I don't think he meant them to do so by looking into each other's eyes.

Jesus celebrated life and he declared all wholesome things good. We are meant to enjoy fruitful relations, good food and refreshing recreation.

Above all, Jesus never puts people down but always raises them up. Notice how Jesus was able to get someone like Mary Magdalene to become one of the greatest saints. He recognized the quality in her that nobody else had noticed – her great capacity to love. Or again, look at how he treats Peter. Remember that Peter denied ever knowing Jesus, not once but three times. After his resurrection, far from rejecting Peter, Jesus entrusts him with his own ministry of service and sacrifice – 'Feed my sheep.'

Bishop Stephen and the Church in Stepney have the privilege of living and teaching the gospel in some of the most deprived communities in the country. Yet, in my experience, that is precisely where the Christian community, living in a tough and hostile environment, does the finest work and always with few resources. It is here that the gospel has the power to restore our humanity and inform that essential vision of faith, justice and peace.

When the report *Faith in the City* was published, particular attention was paid to a training course in Stepney for lay people, called 'Step by Step'. Today it still continues, though now it is called 'New Step'. The course is designed to teach the basic building blocks of the

Christian faith to people with little formal education. More importantly, it recognizes that formal education and intelligence are not the same thing and thereby treats people and their life experiences with absolute seriousness, for they have within them hidden skills and new insights into truth. Above all, New Step, and other courses like Alpha and Emmaus, are designed to build up confidence so that people can begin to explore their sense of discipleship and take on tasks of responsibility and leadership in the Church and community. There could be no more pressing task for the Church today as mischievous powers attempt to undermine, scoff and denigrate the faith of Jesus Christ.

I am delighted to be able to commend Bishop Stephen's book, which will be an enormous help to people becoming familiar with fundamental Christian writings. It is often too easy to talk down to people in attempting to open up demanding texts. Bishop Stephen has avoided any attempt to patronize the reader but rather respects and honours the desire to learn and grow on the pilgrimage of faith. It is at the very heart of the gospel of Jesus Christ that every person, irrespective of background, colour or gender, is treated with dignity and respect. For some two thousand years these writings have been guiding stars for succeeding generations. For all of us they still have the power to direct our steps and lead us on.

✠ Desmond Tutu
Easter 2005

Introduction

In recent years there has been a dramatic increase in the number of courses which provide a basic introduction to the Christian faith. Alpha and Emmaus courses have not only spread round the world, they have also become an important resource for chaplains serving in prisons, colleges and the armed forces.

In part this has come about in response to a growing number of adults articulating a wistful curiosity about the Christian faith, and in part it is the recognition that no longer can it be assumed people have much Christian understanding.

In 1995 a report entitled *On the Way* recommended that the Christian community should take much more seriously the needs of people coming for help in beginning their own journey of faith. It was proposed that the most effective way forward would be by integrating teaching, worship, reflection and pastoral care into a coherent process.

The report recommended that Jesus' Summary of the Law, the Lord's Prayer, the Apostles' Creed and the Beatitudes might provide the necessary material for those exploring their own discipleship. Not only are these important texts for every Christian to learn and make their own, but they might also provide a liturgical focus, read as part of a short act of worship before a study group or within public worship, as those exploring their faith begin to discover their own discipleship prior to baptism and confirmation. Discipleship is a process, not a single event, and these texts give shape, content and direction to the emerging sense of spiritual exploration and confidence.

On this pilgrimage of faith the Christian disciple is urged to travel light. No purse or sandals (Luke 10.4), no gold or silver (Matthew 10.9). Maybe just the Good Book, a little bread to be broken and some wine to be shared.

It is all too easy to carry unnecessary baggage. These four texts, rather than a burden to bear, are really like a break in the trees, a bend in the road or the crest of a hill, all vantage points from which a new vista opens up on the journey.

The Lord's Prayer introduces a pattern of praying by exploring what it means to call God 'Father' and to pray for the coming of the kingdom. Jesus' Summary of the Law involves examining the content of the Ten Commandments. It provides a useful introduction to such words as 'grace' and 'covenant' and opens up issues of moral concern. The Apostles' Creed is a way into historic formulations of faith. The Beatitudes are an opportunity to learn to recognize signs of the kingdom and what the kingdom, with all its radical claims, might actually be like.

None of these texts is self-contained and all of them overlap at one point or another. Whenever possible, Bible references have been given so that alongside these texts something can be learned of the wider background and resource of the Scriptures.

It is often said that faith is caught and not taught. There is great truth in this, but it is not the whole truth. Whether faith is caught from the inspiring example of a friend or the devotions of parents, it is always with the spark of the Holy Spirit. But the faith that is caught still needs to be nurtured and developed. Jesus reminded his disciples to love God not only with all their heart and soul but also with all their mind and strength.

The pages of this book are an invitation not just to think carefully about what is believed but also to pray deeply about the meaning and practice of the Christian faith.

Travelling on the motorway we see those signs which read 'Tiredness kills'. In the busy and frantic world many of us know, there is an exhaustion which can so easily kill the human spirit. Getting through the day or surviving the next crisis at work reduces life to the level of mere existence. So alongside prayer and study I make a plea for you to take time to rest and be still. These pages are not intended as boxes to be ticked or mere information to be absorbed. Rather, in that spirit of rest and reflection, I hope they may be the means by which you are nurtured and strengthened on your own pilgrimage of faith.

First and foremost, discipleship is the response to the call of Jesus, '*Come, follow me.*' From that moment discipleship is a journey of discovery in company with others: '*You did not choose me, but I chose you*' (John 15.16).

On those occasions when you can stop by the way, I hope you will be able to see through these pages something of the glory of the vista set out as far as the human eye can see.

✠ Stephen J. Oliver
Feast of the Conversion of Saint Paul, 2005

Acknowledgements

Brother Jason SSF, my chaplain and personal assistant, has constructed these pages with his customary patience, persistence and humour. I am glad to be able to express my gratitude to him for he is numbered among those to whom this book is dedicated.

The author and publisher gratefully acknowledge permission to reproduce the following copyright material:

on p. 25, the Lord's Prayer as it appears in *Common Worship: Services and Prayers for the Church of England* (Church House Publishing, 2000) is copyright © The English Language Liturgical Consultation and is reproduced by permission of the publisher.

on p. 65, Timothy Rees, 'God is love'.

on p. 66, W. H. Vanstone, 'A Hymn to Creation', from *Love's Endeavour, Love's Expense*, Darton, Longman & Todd, 1977.

on p. 92, Extract from Methodist Covenant Service, taken from the *Methodist Worship Book*, © 1999 Trustees for Methodist Church Purposes. Used by permission of Methodist Publishing House.

Jesus' Summary of the Law

Our Lord Jesus Christ said that the first commandment is this:
'Hear, O Israel, the Lord our God is the only Lord.
You shall love the Lord your God with all your heart,
with all your soul, with all your mind,
and with all your strength.'

The second is this:
'Love your neighbour as yourself.'
There is no other commandment greater than these.
On these two commandments hang all the law and the prophets.

The rule of love

A key word in the somewhat confused culture of Western society is the magic mantra of 'choice'. 'Choice' reflects prosperity and speaks of abundance. 'Choice' is a sign of wealth and independence, since everyone knows that only poor people have no choice. They get what they are given – if they are given anything at all.

So in a world of many choices it might come as a surprise to discover that following the way of Jesus Christ is not about making a lifestyle choice or a career decision. In fact, discipleship is not entirely about choice at all. First and foremost it is a response to the call of Jesus of Nazareth, 'Come, follow me.'

To answer that call and take the first step of faith is to begin a lifetime journey exploring the mystery of God and growing into the maturity of the stature of Jesus Christ. It is a journey of personal challenge and exhilarating freedom.

It is a common misconception that to become a disciple of Jesus Christ means being bound by a whole lot of laws and commandments. As it happens, Jesus distilled the Law of the Old Testament scriptures into just two commandments – love God and love your neighbour as yourself. Both of them are easy enough to say but take a lifetime to put into practice. The call of Jesus is not to an infantile obedience to a set of club rules but to a mature humanity that is free to love. Jeremy Bentham, the eighteenth-century English philosopher, wrote that 'every law is contrary to liberty'. Christian discipleship is not bound by the letter of the law but, as Saint Paul pointed out, is led by the Spirit of God:

> *For you were called to freedom, brothers and sisters, only do not use your freedom as an opportunity for self-indulgence, but through love become slaves to one another. For the whole law is summed up in a single commandment, 'You shall love your neighbour as yourself.'*
>
> (Galatians 5.13–14)

A moral universe

There are those who believe that human behaviour is largely determined by our genes. They might allow for certain modifications to evolve within a specific social context, but essentially they would argue that human freedom, and that includes the freedom to make moral choices, is an illusion.

Then there are those who would argue that any notion of ethics should always be modified in the light of human need or scientific pragmatism. Of course it is wrong to kill, but when a person with a terminal disease is in the last stages and suffering acute distress, surely it is not murder but an act of mercy to put an end to it . . . or him . . . or her? Or again, no one feels entirely comfortable with the idea of genetic engineering, especially with human genes, but the benefits in discovering new treatments for a host of illnesses are held to be sufficient justification. These are areas of fierce moral and social debate. There are no easy answers.

Others would point to areas of human activity where normal ethical concerns might be suspended. Business has sometimes acted in this way when the moral high ground has been sacrificed for the sake of the economic bottom line. Some have acted as if ethical concerns are a kind of optional extra. Nice if you can afford them, but not essential.

Edward Tenner of Princeton University published a book eight years ago with the striking title *Why Things Bite Back*. Basically he was pointing out that just when we think we have solved one problem, we find we have created a few more.

Antibiotics have undoubtedly been the miracle drugs of the twentieth century. However, using them indiscriminately has made them less effective and now we face a rise in 'superbugs', against which we have only a very thin line of defence and soon may have no defence at all.

The blindingly obvious 'law of unforeseen consequences' is all around us. Tenner quoted a hundred examples of why human ingenuity is perpetually creating unexpected new problems after the old ones have apparently been solved.

All this suggests we live in a world of consequences. In Newtonian physics this is expressed in the proposition that for every action there is a reaction. Yet cause and effect, in a predictive sense, breaks down at the sub-atomic level of quantum physics where an action (shining light on a particle) will have an effect, but it will be unpredictable. It is called the Uncertainty Principle. Sometimes it is clear that breaking the code of law has a direct and obvious consequence for the perpetrator. At other times there is a more complex series of consequences, some of them hidden, until the outcome appears further down the line. For this reason, there is a collective social responsibility for ethical issues and not just an individual moral responsibility. Or, as Desmond Tutu expressed it, 'My humanity is bound up with yours, for we can only be human together.'

The decisions human beings make and the actions they take have an effect. That effect is not always predictable (why cannot I do right for doing wrong?) but there is an effect. Interestingly, when a virtual or imaginary world is created, for example in a television 'soap', it is usually the case that the soap reflects a moral world of consequences following on from a certain kind of behaviour. Stealing might not be punished immediately but its effect is seen as the story unfolds. It is this moral world which makes the story more interesting and believable.

Understanding consequences

When it comes to ethical issues it is not always easy to track the consequences of a particular action in a simple cause-and-effect way. But that is very far from saying there is no effect. It might be said that unethical behaviour damages the moral fabric of the universe in ways not always understood. Sometimes innocent people suffer as a result. It is one of the great questions to have exercised the human mind.

Why does the way of the guilty prosper?
Why do all who are treacherous thrive?
(Jeremiah 12.1)

In more recent times businesses have come to realize that a decline in ethical awareness has been very costly to their public image, employee morale and relations with investment partners. They too have learned that they live in a world of consequences.

To live in a world of consequences means that it is not entirely foolish to claim that we live in a moral universe – that is to say, a universe rigged in such a way that moral concerns are not just an optional extra but built into the way things are.

In fact, a sense of moral purpose gives shape and meaning to life beyond simply enjoying the beauty of creation or a 'gritted teeth' mentality of merely surviving. We all know people who would rather make sure of their misery than risk being happy.

The film director Michael Winner tells an amusing story of walking along a beach in Barbados with John Cleese. The sun was shining and the flowers were blooming. Golden sands, a shimmering sea and a cooling breeze. And as they walked John Cleese said, 'You know, Michael, there must be more to life than this.'

Just as the physical universe has been mapped by the so-called laws of physics, so down the centuries human activity has been mapped by so-called moral law. The codes of this law have not only shaped human behaviour and provided the foundation for social cultures, they have also given expression to fundamental human values. In other words, to believe that this life is a free-for-all, where anything goes, is to ignore the law of unforeseen consequences. In fact, it is to deny that we live in a world of consequences at all. And that, in itself, is not a stance of spiritual maturity. Only very young children and naive adolescents behave as if they can do anything with no consequences to follow.

The question, then, is not 'What laws do we need?' but 'What values and what purpose do we believe our ultimate concern to be?' And the answer will have consequences for the way we live. Holding high moral values, however, is no guarantee that either individuals or societies will keep them. We are fallen creatures in a fallen world. There is perversity in the human heart. But even when we fall, there is still that innate sense of right and wrong, of justice and life redeemed.

The civil rights leader Martin Luther King Jr delivered a memorable speech on the steps of the Lincoln Memorial in Washington DC on 28 August 1963. In that speech he shared his dream that his 'four children will one day live in a nation where they will not be judged by the colour of their skin but by the content of their character'.

Twenty-five years later, I went to interview his four children in Atlanta, Georgia, for a documentary programme called *The Legacy of the Dream*.

In the course of conversation his eldest son told me that he vividly remembered his father teaching him that the ultimate test of a man or woman is not where you stand on positions of comfort and convenience but where you stand on positions of challenge and controversy.

'On some questions', he said, 'cowardice asks: is a position safe? Expediency asks: is a position politic? Vanity asks: is a position popular? But conscience asks: is a position right? Sometimes we must take a position that is neither safe, nor popular, nor politic, but conscience tells us it is right.'

This is a good description of what might be called the moral high ground.

Moral codes of law can give expression to this sense of conscience, but the letter of the law is never enough by itself.

In the pilgrimage of faith and in our spiritual evolution, the letter of the law requires a new spirit for its ultimate fulfilment.

The Old Testament Scriptures and the Law of God

A lot of people will have heard of the Ten Commandments even if they cannot recite them. Yet these commandments are just the tip of a very large iceberg. The Law books of the Bible actually contain 659 commandments, which means that the chances are you are likely to be breaking one of them – or at least thinking about it!

All these commandments cover everything from personal property to public hygiene and are largely to be found in the first five books of the Bible. The Jewish name for these books is 'The Law'; in Hebrew, the word is *Tôrâ*.

The original sense of *Tôrâ* is far wider than a set of rules or what is commonly understood by 'law'. The word means instruction, teaching or guidance for a fully human life made possible by the gift of God. So, for example, the word *tôrâ* is used for teaching given by parents to their children (Proverbs 1.8) or by a prophet in rebuking his wayward people (Isaiah 1.10).

These Law books are layered history, like sediment gradually settling in a river bed. They contain different kinds of law (constitutional, criminal, religious) laid down and collected together over a long period of time before being shaped into their present literary form. They are not unique. Several collections of laws are known from ancient Mesopotamia. The most famous is the Code of Hammurabi of Babylon from the eighteenth century BC, now exhibited in Paris at the Louvre.

However, in one important respect the Law books of the Old Testament scriptures are quite distinctive. The story of God giving the Law to Moses (Exodus 20.1–17) means that the Law itself is sacred. To keep the Law is a religious obligation, not simply a civic duty.

Since the Law came from God then the Law itself has the potential to say something about the character of God. Take, for example, the law concerning a cloak accepted as security for a loan. The law evokes sensitive kindness and reveals God to be the God of compassion and mercy.

> *If you take your neighbour's cloak in pawn, you shall restore it before the sun goes down; for it may be your neighbour's only clothing to use as cover; in what else shall that person sleep? And if your neighbour cries out to me, I will listen, for I am compassionate.* (Exodus 22.26–7)

On the whole, biblical law goes further than other legal codes in making provision for the disadvantaged in society, the resident foreigner, widows and orphans. There is a commandment not to scour the fields during the harvest but to leave the edges for others to glean:

> *When you reap the harvest of your land you shall not reap to the very edges of your field . . . You shall leave them for the poor and the alien; I am the LORD your God.* (Leviticus 19.9–10)

Later on in the Bible, the beautiful story of Ruth tells how a young widow is able to feed herself and her mother-in-law from the pickings of just such a field. So God the Creator, who provides 'every green plant for food' (Genesis 1.30), is seen to be the same God of mercy and compassion who provides for the poor and hungry by means of the sacred Law.

God and the covenant

The giving of the Law to Moses is only part of the story. The Law is the basis of the covenant, the relationship between God and his chosen people. God kept faith with his people, delivering them from slavery in Egypt and leading them to the Promised Land. For their part the people promised obedience to the Law. At the heart of that covenant relationship are the 'Ten Words', more commonly known as the 'Ten Commandments'. For many people the Ten Commandments (if they know them at all) are the foundation on which every civilized society is built. After all, it is unthinkable that any community could survive by tolerating theft, murder and deceit!

'The Covenant' is a fundamental conviction of the Old Testament Scriptures. A covenant establishes a solemn relationship between two parties. It can be made between two individuals:

> *Then Jonathan made a covenant with David, because he loved him as his own soul.* (1 Samuel 18.3)

or between husband and wife:

> *The LORD was a witness between you and the wife of your youth, to whom you have been faithless, though she is your companion and your wife by covenant.* (Malachi 2.14)

More significantly, in the ancient world an emperor might draw up an agreement with vassal states within the empire. This agreement might include a list of duties in return for the protection and benevolence of the emperor. Such an agreement would be read in public from time to time, reminding the people of their obligations. It is important to note that an agreement of this kind is not an agreement between two equal parties. This 'covenant' simply outlines the foundation of the relationship as one of duties and obligations. Renege on these obligations and the entire relationship is broken.

Although there are several examples of God establishing a covenant relationship with Noah or Abraham or David, there is no doubt that the controlling covenant is that established at Mount Sinai (or Horeb) in the giving of the Law brought about through the faith and obedience of Moses. Yet the initiative for establishing this covenant relationship always lies with God.

God's saving initiative is revealed in the mighty act of redemption:

> *It is because the LORD loved you, and kept the oath which he swore to your ancestors, that the LORD has brought you out with a mighty hand, and redeemed you from the house of slavery, from the hand of Pharaoh king of Egypt.* (Deuteronomy 7.8)

11

And the seal on this saving initiative, this mighty act, is the covenant promise, 'I will be your God and you shall be my people.' It is that relationship which is founded on faithfulness in keeping the Law.

In years to come, when the life of the people of God was threatened by corruption within or invasion from foreign armies, the great prophets would expose the broken covenant and call the people to repentance and back to the covenant promise (Amos 3, Hosea 2 and Jeremiah 7). Yet the people proved unfaithful, breaking the covenant by failing to keep the Law. Again and again God calls them but,

> *The more I called them,*
> *the more they went from me;*
> *they kept sacrificing to the Baals,*
> *and offering incense to idols.*
>   (Hosea 11.2)

Failure to keep the Law led to the corruption of those in power, and in the end to their own destruction:

> *Alas for those who devise wickedness*
> *and evil deeds on their beds!*
> *When the morning dawns, they perform it,*
> *because it is in their power.*
>   (Micah 2.1)

When, in recent years, a senior politician was caught out in a particular act of betrayal and was asked why he did it, he could find no reason other than to say, 'I did it because I could.' Evil has an insidious power to corrupt from within.

Even here there is a profound sense of God revealing new insights to those with eyes to see. The prophets were aware of the danger of a narrow legalism which would lead to spiritual stagnation. They began to look to the faithfulness of God restoring a new relationship, a new covenant, with the law no longer written on tablets of stone but inscribed on the human heart.

> *I will put my law within them and I will write it on their hearts; and*
> *I will be their God, and they shall be my people.*   (Jeremiah 31.33)

The Ten Commandments

The three world faiths, Judaism, Christianity and Islam, have all, to a greater or lesser degree, embraced the Ten Commandments as a common basic ethic. Not as some kind of optional extra, but as essential to the wellbeing of every human society. It is not for nothing that we talk of law *and* order. When law breaks down, order collapses into chaos. Nor is it for nothing that God's act of creation brings order out of chaos. Only in an ordered world can life and creativity truly flourish. The Ten Commandments are the basic framework of an ordered society.

The first commandments relate to the ultimate inescapable reality of the mystery of God from which all else flows.

'**I am the LORD your God, who brought you out of the land of Egypt, out of the house of slavery . . .**' God is God of mystery and majesty that no human mind can fathom. God, who chooses to reveal himself in the mighty act of redemption which brought his people out of slavery and led them to freedom.

'**You shall have no other gods before me.**' No one and nothing can lay greater claim to the allegiance of the human heart. No earthly power, no contemporary 'ism' – monetarism, socialism, nationalism, conservatism. Nothing and no one can put themselves above the law of God.

'**You shall not make for yourself an idol . . .**' A society which speaks glibly of pop idols and the cult of celebrity simply reflects the age-old human temptation to worship gods made in our own image. The primary and ultimate concern here is with the sense of the sacred.

'**You shall not make wrongful use of the name of the LORD your God.**' The world faiths of Judaism and Islam have a profound sense of the holy, whereby even the name of God is to be avoided altogether or spoken only with deep reverence. For if God is not holy then our very sense of the sacred is eroded. What then is sacred? The earth which gives life and which is treated with such disdain? Marriage and the family? Human life itself? If God is not sacred, then the sanctity of anything is undermined and what was once believed to be inviolable becomes just another expendable part of the culture of convenience. Blasphemy erodes the very notion of the sacred, the inviolable and the holy.

'**Remember the sabbath day and keep it holy.**' This commandment is the one with serious implications for social cohesion and personal welfare. The human resources department of a large national institution once commissioned research to find out the optimum length of time people could work while retaining their energy and efficiency. At great financial cost a heavy document was produced with the result. The bottom line revealed the outcome – six days' work with one day's proper rest! Somebody could have saved themselves a great deal of money and effort.

The so-called 'Protestant work ethic' is often blamed for creating the conditions for people to work too hard. It is widely misunderstood. Far from encouraging people to work long hours, the Protestant work ethic took the Sabbath commandment with absolute seriousness and ensured, even at the height of the manic drive of industrialization, that people had a proper day off for rest with their families. Sunday shopping, whatever its convenience, has destroyed much of that Sabbath rest. For many people the consequences will be exhaustion, mental stress and even less chance of proper family life. Of course, people have to work in essential services on the Sabbath, but the principle of Sabbath rest for society and for individuals is discarded at our peril.

Almost by extension the next commandment relates to family life.

'**Honour your father and mother**.' Each generation grows up being cared for by the previous generation until the time comes when the tables are turned and the older generation needs care and nurture. The health and humanity of any society is measured by the way older people are treated. 'Respect and care for them as you will want to be treated one day' is a useful maxim for every generation – or, as the last part of this commandment puts it, 'that you too may live long in the land the Lord your God is giving you'.

Three commandments follow concerned with the life of the community. In one way or another they are about mutual trust.

'**You shall not murder**' is clearly about the sacredness of human life and inviolable respect for each person. It is not just about wilful murder but also about safety at work or careful driving. We all have another person's life in our hands from time to time.

'**You shall not commit adultery**' is, of course, concerned to protect the sanctity of marriage but also speaks of the need for integrity in all human relationships. After all, betrayal destroys confidence and trust quicker than anything.

'You shall not steal' is obvious enough, though it seems big business needs reminding that this commandment also condemns those who plunder pension funds or con the poor with shoddy goods!

'You shall not bear false witness against your neighbour.' Speaking the truth is the foundation of trust. Telling lies, spreading unfounded rumours and speculating in idle gossip is corrosive of all human relationships. In Las Vegas there are many casinos. They are vast places, filled with all kinds of gambling games. There are no windows. It is easy to wander in but for obvious reasons there are few signs to help you leave. When you are cut off from the world outside, the effect is to blur the boundary between reality and fantasy. The punter spending any amount of time in this artificial world loses all reference to the real world and cannot even tell whether it is night or day. Spreading lies and living in a world of falsehood is to lose touch with reality. But truth will out and finally the whole fantasy collapses. As one wise sage put it, 'The problem with lies is that you have to remember what you said!'

> *O what a tangled web we weave,*
> *When first we practise to deceive.*
> (Sir Walter Scott)

And the final commandment:

'You shall not covet your neighbour's house, you shall not covet your neighbour's wife, or male or female slave, or ox, or donkey, or anything that belongs to your neighbour.' Covetousness is the most insidious of sins because at first it goes unrecognized. It cloaks itself in other more noble aspirations, such as ambition or an aspiration for a better life. Yet in truth covetousness is rooted in envy. It not only desires what someone else has, it comes to want it even though it might involve murder, theft or adultery. In its most pernicious form it is so consumed with what others have that it makes a person blind to the blessings in their own life. They are reduced to the misery of discontent, unrelieved by the graciousness of a grateful heart.

So there we have it. Ten Commandments, which from ancient times have mapped out the moral high ground, not just for Jews but for many peoples. On the face of it, quite straightforward. However, trying to keep these commandments in the diverse and complex situations most people face from time to time means that serious questions soon start to be asked. 'You shall not murder.' Does that include capital punishment? Were the rebellious German officers who tried to kill Hitler in the darkest days of the Second World War breaking this commandment? What about euthanasia? Does this mean pacifism is the only right response to a malevolent and evil threat?

Or take this example. As you are walking down the street, a man with a terrified look on his face runs past you and down a side street. Seconds later, another man runs up with a knife in his hand, demanding to know which street the first man had taken. Do you tell the truth and thereby help one man to stab another, or do you lie? Absolute law is always open to the challenge of exceptional situations. So the Law over time becomes modified and greater detail is added as new cases are brought before the lawyers for their opinion.

Going further

It has also to be said that the Law in these terms falls short of any recognizable Christian ethic. Nothing is said of loving those who hate you and no claim is made that love knows no limit to its endurance. On the contrary, the Law seeks to be precise and proceeds by defining obligation and duty. Love your neighbour is good, but soon, very soon, someone is going to ask, 'And who is my neighbour?'

It is precisely this question which is asked of Jesus by a lawyer trying to justify himself. The question is put in the hope that, by defining the term 'neighbour', some kind of limit will be placed on the obligation to love. In other words, the Law would only expect love to be exercised in the context of a precisely defined set of circumstances. Jesus responds by telling the story of the Good Samaritan (Luke 10.25–37).

It is a carefully constructed story. The hero is not a Jew but a Samaritan. Jews and Samaritans did not get on, to put it mildly. An equivalent story might be told of a Protestant man beaten and left for dead in Belfast at the height of the sectarian violence, only to be rescued and helped by a Catholic man going down the same street. Jesus refuses to give a definition of a neighbour but simply describes a situation where kindness, mercy and gracious generosity save a person in desperate need. Jesus turns the question on its head. 'Who do you think was a neighbour to the man who fell into the hands of robbers?' The lawyer said, 'The one who showed him mercy.' Your neighbour is anyone in need of the help you can give. There is no statute of limitation, only opportunity of service.

While laws can go some way to limiting the harmful and destructive side of human nature, there is a boundary to what they can achieve. Damage limitation is one thing, the promotion of what is good and life-giving is quite another.

In more recent times lawyers have been quick to see the proper establishment and exercise of law as being key to the development of independent African nations. Professor Antony Allott spent 32 years analysing what the law was and did before publishing, in 1980, a book entitled *The Limits of Law*, which set out what the law did not and could not do. He addressed the fundamental question of how the law can be used to build the society that people seek. However, he recognized that when the law is abused or overloaded it can foster discontent and risks becoming counterproductive by collapsing into lawlessness. There are clear constraints to what the law, by itself, can achieve.

Jesus' Summary of the Law

You can imagine that in the course of time laws became ever more detailed as they were interpreted to cover more and more cases. Remembering that to keep the Law was, for a Jew, a religious obligation, not simply a civic duty, you can begin to understand that the Law became even more a burden to bear and a barrier to a close and right relationship with God. No surprise, then, that Jesus could use harsh language when it came to lawyers:

> *Woe also to you lawyers! For you load people with burdens hard to bear, and you yourselves do not lift a finger to ease them.* (Luke 11.46)

However, if there was a tendency to make laws ever more detailed, there was also a pull in the opposite direction to distil from the Law a summary which could act as a controlling principle from which the whole Law might subsequently be derived.

Rabbi Hillel, for example, in the first century AD is said to have taught: 'What is hateful to yourself, do not do to your neighbour; this is the whole law, the rest is commentary!'

There is every reason to believe that Jesus took the Law with absolute seriousness: 'Do not think I have come to abolish the law or the prophets; I have come not to abolish but to fulfil' (Matthew 5.17).

It is perfectly reasonable, therefore, that on one occasion a scribe should come to Jesus with a serious question: 'Which commandment is the first of all?' (Mark 12.28–34).

Jesus' response is instructive. First and foremost he recites the words by which every Jewish person acknowledges the mystery of God. It is said every time a faithful Jew leaves or returns home, enters or departs from the synagogue. It is written on a small scroll and placed in the mezuzah, fixed to the right-hand door-post of the house where it can be clearly seen. It is known by its opening word in Hebrew as the *Shema* – 'Hear'.

> *Hear, O Israel: the* LORD *is our God, the* LORD *alone.*
> (Deuteronomy 6.4)

This is the source from which all else flows. The whole of the Law comes from God, reveals his nature and is an instrument of his sacred purpose. If God is one, then there follows a divine unity and fundamental wholeness of being throughout creation. If God is one, then there is a divine unity and fundamental wholeness intended for all humanity, irrespective of gender, colour, race or any other instrument of discrimination.

The first call on the creation must be response to the source of all that is:

> *You shall love the* LORD *your God with all your heart, with all your soul, with all your mind and with all your strength.* (cf. Deuteronomy 6:5)

There are several Greek words for love. Imagine someone writing these sentences – 'John loves Mavis', 'Harold loves his father', 'Mary loves her friends.' English has only one word for love but the Greeks would have used *eros* for John loving Mavis; *storge* for Harold's love of his father; *philia* for Mary's love of her friends.

Yet there is another word which the early Christians used to describe the kind of love that goes beyond romance, family and friends. It is the love that does not have to be earned but flows out spontaneously and generously to the unlikeable as well as the like-able, to the wicked as well as to the good. The word is *agape*. It is used of God's love for the whole of creation and is seen in all that Jesus said and did. It is there in his gracious embrace of the sinner, his healing of the sick and his welcome for the outcast. This is love, *agape*, in action.

The first commandment is therefore to love God in response to the outpouring of love God first showed in the glory of creation and embodied in Jesus Christ. There is little distinction to be made between heart and soul and mind and strength. In Hebrew the heart is where the will is exercised, not where the emotions are to be found. The point is clear. The commandment is to love God with every fibre of being, with strength of will, clarity of mind and depth of soul.

Since faith and ethics, belief and behaviour, are so bound to-gether in the ancient Law, it follows that the second commandment is this:

> *Love your neighbour as yourself.*
> (Leviticus 19.18)

Again, the word for love is *agape*, the love that does not need to be earned but flows spontaneously for the prosperity and wellbeing of another.

Neither commandment can be separated from the other. To love God is to love your neighbour. To love your neighbour is to love God. 'On these two commandments hang all the law and the prophets.'

It is precisely in this mutual giving and receiving of love that the purpose of the Law is fulfilled. For here is God's nature revealed as love, and here love is the instrument of God's purpose.

This is the foundation of the new covenant between God and his people. No longer is it a covenant relationship based on the demands of the Law. Here is the new creation built on the covenant of God's self-giving, sacrificial love in Jesus Christ.

When a person does wrong and commits sin – as we all do – God does not say, 'It doesn't matter.' It does matter. However, God does say, 'It will not destroy our relationship. Even if you crucify me, I will not leave you or abandon you.' That is the measure and mystery of the love of God embodied in Jesus Christ. The life-giving Spirit of Jesus has replaced the letter of the Law. Or as Saint Augustine famously put it:

Love . . . and do as you like.

Just as something of the nature of God was expressed in the Law, so the nature and purpose of God find a living expression in Jesus of Nazareth – his life of love, his self-giving sacrifice, his life-giving resurrection.

Jesus came to liberate people from fear into freedom. The way to lay claim to that freedom is through faith. Many people believe the opposite of faith is doubt. In truth, the opposite to faith is fear. Time and time again Jesus is heard to say, 'Do not be afraid' – 'Fear not'.

The freedom to which he calls people is the freedom to risk faith and love and grow in that true humanity measured by nothing less than the stature of Jesus himself. To this end Jesus treats his disciples as growing in maturity. If there is a template for discipleship, it is not a set of instructions but the pattern of his own life.

The words bequeathed to us in his summary of the Law are not a street map, forcing us down a particular road, but a compass giving us the direction to travel. And this was always the broader meaning of *tôrâ* – not simply a set of detailed rules but, rather, instruction, teaching and guidance. It could not be otherwise. Many of the critical issues facing society today were totally unknown two thousand years ago. Street maps rapidly become obsolete. Following the compass bearing and working out our own salvation in fear and trembling is faith in practice and freedom indeed.

The law indeed was given through Moses; grace and truth came through Jesus Christ. No one has ever seen God. It is God the only Son who is close to the Father's heart, who has made him known. (John 1.17–18)

How it works

It is very interesting to see how the rule of love comes to be expressed. Whereas the commandments of the Law are largely in a negative form, determining behaviour by prohibition, the law of love is expressed in positive terms, encouraging what can be done with a gracious Spirit. Not 'you shall not', but rather, 'you shall . . .'

Some of this graciousness can be seen in Paul's letter to the Romans:

Contribute to the needs of the saints; extend hospitality to strangers. Bless those who persecute you; bless and do not curse them.

(Romans 12.13–14)

The injunction to extend hospitality to strangers was the historic foundation of monastic hospitality, the beginning of hospitals and hospices.

Today there is much talk of our society needing to be tolerant, when, actually, frightened refugees and genuine asylum seekers require more than to be tolerated. Hospitality is the human capacity to make welcome, with all that implies of providing food, shelter and the dignity of work.

In the letter to the Hebrews this sense of positive provision can be seen even more clearly. Instead of a prohibition against adultery, there is the commendation:

> *Let marriage be held in honour by all.*
> (Hebrews 13.4)

The Christian community is urged to remember those in prison and those who are being tortured. Evil and suffering are not just to be avoided but must be confronted and overcome.

The letter to the Ephesians is often the subject of much criticism for seeming to place women in an inferior position, but nevertheless uses positive language.

> *Husbands, love your wives, just as Christ loved the church and gave himself up for her.* (Ephesians 5.25)

In fact, with regard to husbands the letter goes even further:

> *Husbands should love their wives as they do their own bodies. He who loves his wife loves himself.* (Ephesians 5.28)

But then this should come as no surprise, since what is seen here is the early Christian community working out in practice exactly what Jesus had taught his first disciples as part of the law of love:

> *Love your neighbour as yourself.*

Questions

1 What do you think are the limitations of law?
2 What do you understand by the 'law of love'?
3 Is the 'golden rule' – do to others what you would like them to do to you – enough guidance in today's complex world?
4 What is the value of the Ten Commandments today?
5 Do you love yourself enough to love your neighbour?

The Lord's Prayer

Our Father in heaven,
hallowed be your name,
your kingdom come,
your will be done,
on earth as in heaven.
Give us today our daily bread.
Forgive us our sins
as we forgive those
who sin against us.
Lead us not into temptation
but deliver us from evil.
For the kingdom, the power,
and the glory are yours
now and for ever. Amen.

Our Father, who art in heaven,
hallowed be thy name;
thy kingdom come;
thy will be done;
on earth as it is in heaven.
Give us this day our daily bread.
and forgive us our trespasses,
as we forgive those
who trespass against us.
And lead us not into temptation;
but deliver us from evil.
For thine is the kingdom,
the power, and the glory,
for ever and ever. Amen.

Saint Paul's Cathedral in London welcomes many thousands of tourist visitors in the course of a year. On the hour, every hour, a chaplain will lead a short interlude of prayer ending with the invitation to join together saying the 'Our Father', 'Pater Noster', 'Vater Unser', 'Padre Nostro', or 'Notre Père'. By whatever name it is known, the Lord's Prayer is familiar to those of many nations and languages. There is even a dedicated website on the Internet which claims to have the Lord's Prayer in 1,310 languages and dialects. Among all these is the version in Aramaic, the very words that Jesus would have taught his friends:

aboon dabashmacya
Our Father in heaven
nethkadash shamal
holy is his name

So universal is this prayer that there are those who claim that its rhythm and cadences remain very similar no matter which language is being spoken.

Even in English there are different versions, and that is not surprising in a prayer so rich in meaning and very often learned by reciting it aloud. Cliff Richard sang the words to the tune of 'Auld Lang Syne' at the turn of the millennium. Gracie Fields, the popular singer from Rochdale, sang the words to soldiers serving in the Far East when the announcement was made that the Second World War had finally ended on 2 September 1945. It is a universal prayer known throughout the world and prayed down the centuries.

There is nothing in the words that a devout Jew or Muslim could not pray with integrity. Carl Jung, the eminent Swiss psychiatrist, might say that the prayer is so universal that it resonates deep within the collective unconscious, even when individuals can only call to mind half-remembered phrases.

Learning a prayer by repetition and passing it on by word of mouth probably accounts for some of the differences in various versions of the Lord's Prayer. Matthew's Gospel (6.9ff) has a longer version than Luke's Gospel (11.2). Each might well have been the version used in the particular worshipping community familiar to Matthew and Luke. Matthew's version feels more liturgical than Luke's but the differences are not of any major spiritual significance. Of more importance is the fact that both Gospels make it clear that this was the way Jesus taught his friends to pray. From very early days, it seems that this prayer was used not just by individual people but collectively, in public worship, by the whole Christian community.

Prayer

Prayer is primitive. At one level it is the most natural and spontaneous response in the world. In moments of ecstasy and times of crisis, there is evidence to suggest people find themselves praying even when they would not claim to be 'religious'. Prayer in these circumstances might be commendably brief – 'Thank God' or 'God help them'. At this level it is more an instinct than a considered decision, but in some mysterious way this instinct to pray is part of what it means to be human.

Nor is it necessary to use fancy words or eloquent language. Indeed, there are times when prayer is most profound when words fail.

It is more than words; more than 'the conscious occupation of the praying mind', as T.S. Eliot says in 'Little Gidding'.

I take it that this is something of what Jesus meant when he taught his disciples not to 'heap up empty phrases . . . for your Father knows what you need before you ask him' (Matthew 6.7–8). Too many words simply get in the way.

If prayer is a basic human response to triumph or tragedy, then it must be said that prayer is dangerous. Without proper understanding there is always the temptation that praying will pander to the immature demands of the child within. This is one reason why prayer is sometimes reduced to the level of 'asking for things'. Prayers in this mode are not necessarily wrong, but usually they need to mature into a deeper experience. Prayer is a conduit of communication and therefore vital to that fundamental personal relationship with God.

All our relationships are a mixture of motives and needs, but there is no denying that the most authentic relationships are found where people affirm each other. By contrast, the most fragile relationships in business, marriage or community are those based on exploitation. In other words, in a mature relationship people are there because they want to be there and not primarily for what they can get out of it as a means of meeting their own exclusive demands.

Prayer used as a magic formula or demanding an act of divine manipulation to meet selfish needs will not work. The Christian faith is quite clear that while all life is dependent on God as the 'whence of our being', that is for our very existence, nonetheless God relates to us with respect for our freedom and by affirming each individual's unique personhood. Respect for freedom and affirming ultimate worth are the two most significant ingredients in any creative relationship with the potential for personal growth. The most profound prayers are not the longest but they are the most perceptive, and they always start not with pleading but with affirmation:

The LORD is my shepherd.
   (Psalm 23)

O LORD our Sovereign,
how majestic is your name in all the earth!
   (Psalm 8.1)

And they acclaim the sovereign freedom of God, trusting that in freedom God will do what is good:

. . . yet not my will but yours be done.
For the kingdom, the power and the glory are yours now and for ever.

So God will not pander to the immature child within but affirms each unique person, calling them into a transforming relationship. To follow Jesus means entering that relationship and growing into his likeness. 'Being transformed into the same likeness' (2 Corinthians 3.18) is one description of discipleship. Do not pray if you do not want to change because prayer is the channel of God's transforming grace. It is risky stuff. Prayer was the means whereby Albert Schweitzer gave up a brilliant academic career to care for those afflicted by leprosy in Africa. Prayer for the 'despis'd slave' sustained

William Wilberforce in the long and arduous struggle to abolish the slave trade.

Prayer is primitive. Prayer is risky, for it can change your life. Prayer also requires courage.

It takes a brave person to resist the brainwashing which in a secular age dismisses prayer as a waste of time – but then, people in other ages sometimes thought like that, only to discover again its mystery and curious attraction. 'What profit do we get if we pray?' (Job 21.15) is a slogan which finds an astonishing echo in a world which constantly asks, 'What is in it for me?'

Considerable courage is required of those who would combat the spiritual bankruptcy of much contemporary cynicism. Yet once the breakthrough is made then patience is needed to recover the skills of waiting, stillness and concentration that have been wasting away because of our obsession with 'doing', 'being occupied', 'keeping busy'.

Many have found that just ten minutes in quiet contemplation or reflective prayer each day has made a world of difference to their whole life.

All of this is but a background to the actual practice of prayer. Jesus taught his friends to pray, since for him and for them it was the most natural thing in the world. Not the easiest, but natural, primitive, just like breathing. He taught them to pray knowing that his prayer was no mere convention. It was subversive, dangerous and transforming. Jesus taught them to pray knowing it would take courage, patience and perseverance. These are exactly the qualities required of any person serious about discipleship. No one can walk the way of Jesus without the sustaining grace which comes in being open to God.

Prayers in the Bible

The Bible is a rich quarry of profound prayers. They contain much wisdom. The book of the prophet Hosea ends with these words of advice:

> *Those who are wise understand these things;*
> *those who are discerning know them.*
>   (Hosea 14.9)

It is to the prophet Hosea that we owe the vivid image of God as the loving Father:

When Israel was a child, I loved him,
and out of Egypt I called my son.

(Hosea 11.1)

Here is the picture of the Father who takes his children in his arms, who feeds them and leads them with compassion. Yet the more God calls them, the further they go from him. When Jesus called God 'Father', and when Paul lays claim to that same form of intimate address,

When we cry 'Abba! Father!'
. . . it is that very Spirit bearing witness . . .
that we are children of God.

(Romans 8.15–16)

somewhere in the background is that picture of the prophet Hosea who knew God, not as a despotic ruler or capricious deity, but as the Father who cares for his children.

Solomon is regarded as a wise king, a person of perceptive judgement. Solomon is invited to ask for anything from God. His prayer is a model of spiritual perception.

And now, O LORD my God, you have made your servant king in place of
my father David, although I am only a little child; I do not know how to
go out or come in . . . Give your servant therefore an understanding mind
to govern your people, able to discern between good and evil.

(1 Kings 3.7–9)

Solomon had the wit to ask for what he knew he needed. It is not necessarily the same as asking for what you want. Solomon's wisdom grew out of his prayer as a gift from God. What is of primary importance is the insight to know what we need. It is this which gives depth to our prayers and wisdom in our lives.

Something of this richness can be seen in the letters of Paul and other early Christian writers. Take the prayer at the beginning of the letter to the Ephesians. Clearly, thanksgiving is a crucial part of praying for others:

I do not cease to give thanks for you as I remember you in my prayers.

(Ephesians 1.16)

A deep sense of thankfulness lies at the heart of all Paul's prayers, a practice we would do well to remember:

Rejoice always, pray without ceasing, give thanks in all circumstances.
(1 Thessalonians 5.16)

It is all too easy to manage our misery by remembering our woes and anxieties. Not so for the spiritual giants who teach us the essential patterns of prayer:

The Lord is near. Do not worry about anything, but in everything by prayer and supplication, with thanksgiving, let your requests be made known to God. (Philippians 4.5–6)

From thanksgiving, the prayer at the beginning of the letter to the Ephesians moves to asking God, not for this or that, but for the deep things of the Spirit.

That . . . God . . . may give you a spirit of wisdom and revelation as you come to know him, so that, with the eyes of your heart enlightened, you may know what is the hope to which he has called you.
(Ephesians 1.17–18)

This is a prayer for the early Christian community in Ephesus, that they may be granted the gift of wisdom. The word for wisdom in Greek is *sophia*, and it means the knowledge of ultimate things or, in a practical way, that they might know the difference between what is important and what is *really* important. It is to make decisions by seeing the world through God's eyes and discerning what is of eternal value, not simply short-term convenience.

To this prayer for wisdom is added the desire for 'revelation as you come to know him'. No one can fully fathom the mystery of God, and the pilgrimage of faith is one of lifelong learning and growing in spiritual stature. This prayer is asking that those early Christian women and men in Ephesus might be open to all that God had yet to teach them of his mercy, grace and truth.

Finally, the prayer asks that 'the eyes of [their] heart[s]' might be enlightened. 'The eyes of your heart' is not a confusion of anatomy. The heart in the ancient world is not, as for us, the place associated with emotion, but rather the centre of the will. 'She put her heart and soul into it' is something which might be said to describe whole-hearted effort and commitment. To pray that the eyes of the heart might be enlightened is a prayer that those early Christians might not only see clearly what they have to do as disciples of Jesus, but also have the will to complete it.

Barely a few lines, but what a rich prayer this is. No wonder that, when Jesus taught his friends how to pray, he should do so not only with an economy of words but also with a depth of meaning.

The Lord's Prayer – Our Father

Some have described the 'Our Father' as a pattern prayer, a kind of model prayer in its structure. It begins with adoration, 'hallowed be your name', moves to petition, 'your kingdom come', acknowledging the primacy of God's will before asking for what we truly need – daily bread to feed us and forgiveness to heal us – before the final ascription of glory, 'for the kingdom, the power and the glory are yours, now and for ever'.

So the prayer begins with phrases of affirmation and honour:

Our Father in heaven,
hallowed be your name . . .

God is acknowledged as no person's private possession. It is prayer not to 'my God' but to 'our Father'. God is the Father of all creation and those who pray can only do so by recognizing that they come to God with all their sisters and brothers.

Those who do not love a brother or sister whom they have seen, cannot
love God whom they have not seen.   (1 John 4.20)

In the same way, those who cannot come with their sisters and brothers cannot expect God to be open to their prayers. 'Our Father' acknowledges the essential unity of all creation under God, recognizing that what affects a part affects the whole. Since God is one ('Hear, O Israel, the LORD our God is one LORD'), then there is an essential unity in creation to which we lay claim in addressing God as 'Our Father'.

The word 'Father' in Hebrew is *Abba*, which some have maintained to be a very intimate form of address, akin to 'Daddy'. Others have tried not to overstate this claim but nonetheless admit it is a very personal form of address. The same rhythm of speech is found in other languages – Abba – Papa – Dada – all of them carrying their own sense of a warm and close relationship of trust and love.

'Father' is not always a happy image for everyone. In particular, those who have experience of a violent and abusive father find it hard to picture God in this way. Yet the image of God as Father goes way back to the time of the prophet Hosea and beyond, as we saw earlier. It is a natural progression to call God 'Father' having known God as Creator, Defender, Sustainer and Redeemer, all attributes revealed in the story of God's people, rescued from slavery in Egypt, fed in the desert and brought to the Promised Land flowing with milk and honey.

In the Psalms, the great spiritual song book of the people of God, there are several interesting phrases:

Father of orphans and protector of widows
is God in his holy habitation.
(Psalm 68.5)

As a father has compassion for his children
so the LORD has compassion for those who fear him.
(Psalm 103.13)

The idea seems to be appealing not so much to the experience of a child in relation to 'Father' but rather to the human experience of what it means to be a father to your own child. As Jesus once taught:

If you then, who are evil, know how to give good gifts to your children,
how much more will your Father in heaven give good things
to those who ask him!
(Matthew 7.11)

Or again, take this from Psalm 89, where God says,

I have exalted one chosen from the people.
I have found my servant David . . .
He shall cry to me, 'You are my Father,
my God, and the rock of my salvation.'
(Psalm 89.19–26)

There is no doubt that Jesus, in calling God 'Abba', 'Father', is drawing on a long-established tradition which in his day was gender-specific. Since God transcends all gender limitations, or rather, since God embraces all gender, the experience of being 'Mother' can equally be an icon for the mystery of God.

No one quite understands the overwhelming feeling of what it is to be 'Mother' or 'Father' until their own child is born. If, then, human parents, with all their limitations, can feel like this, how much more must God's compassion be for his beloved creation?

In fact, the fifteenth-century mystic Julian of Norwich writes eloquently of God as Mother in the *Revelations of Divine Love* and uses the sense of Mother to refer to Jesus:

> *And thus in our creation God almighty is our natural Father, and God all wisdom is our natural Mother . . .*
>
> *In this I saw that all the debts we owe, by God's command, to fatherhood and motherhood by reason of God's fatherhood and motherhood, are repaid in the true loving of God.*
>
> *He willeth then that we use the condition of a child: for when it is hurt or adread, it runneth hastily to the Mother for help with all its might. So willeth he that we do, as a meek child saying this: 'my kind Mother, my Gracious Mother . . . have mercy on me . . .'*
>
> (Chapter 67, *Revelations of Divine Love*)

Much could be written concerning this profound icon of God as Mother and Father but two particular experiences of human parenthood are worth special consideration.

The first is the apparent paradox of bringing up children in order for them to leave home. Every parent who loves their children dearly knows that to love them is to prepare them to lead their own lives, taking responsibility for themselves and growing into their own maturity.

'The world come of age' was Paul Tillich's famous phrase, describing how people outgrow superstition and childish religion on their journey of faith, discarding these false idols, in order to mature in their own personhood and rediscover a more profound spirituality.

> *. . . the process by which the world came of age was an abandonment of a false conception of God, and a clearing of the decks for the God of the Bible, who conquers power and space in the world by his weakness.*
>
> (P. Tillich, *The Courage to Be*, Yale University Press, 1952)

It is, of course, precisely this experience of leaving and returning home to the Father which lies at the heart of Jesus' story of the Prodigal Son (Luke 15.11–32).

It is no exaggeration to claim that with the power of knowledge the future of all life on planet Earth will depend on whether human beings grow in their spiritual maturity or simply exercise an adolescent propensity to exploit freedom without taking any personal responsibility. How to handle power safely is the challenge of the age to our humanity.

The second experience of parenthood to note is the anguish of watching your own child go through times of pain and hurt. Sometimes, hard though it is to stand back, parental intervention is the least helpful thing. But there is hardly a parent in the world watching their own child suffer who would not sacrifice themselves for the sake of their child. If that is a profound experience of human parenthood, how much more so is it a reflection of God's love for his creation?

When Tillich points to the 'God of the Bible, who conquers . . . the world by his weakness' he is pointing us to the God who is revealed in the life and death of Jesus Christ, the God who is the Father of a crucified Son. Nowhere is this relationship more poignantly expressed than in the Garden of Gethsemane on the night before Jesus died, when he prays:

> *Abba, Father, for you all things are possible; remove this cup from me; yet, not what I want, but what you want.* (Mark 14.36)

It is clear that Jesus used the familiar 'Abba', 'Father', in his prayer to God and taught his friends to do the same. By invitation and by example, therefore, all who follow Jesus, by virtue of their baptism, lay claim to call God 'Abba', 'Father', knowing that the Father of Jesus will not abandon them in life or death but wills them to grow up, mature in the stature and likeness of his own beloved Son.

This Father, revealed in the life, death and resurrection of Jesus, is the God whose name is to be honoured, respected, cherished, made holy – hallowed. It is the positive fulfilment of the commandment not to take the name of God in vain and is the opposite of any swearing or blasphemy using the divine name. In this context it is both an affirmation of the holiness of God and a prayer that for the whole of creation the very name of God might be held sacred.

The kingdom

The first petition for the coming of the kingdom is conveyed in the manner of Hebrew poetry, where the first line is repeated in different words but where the meaning is the same:

Your kingdom come
your will be done.

The kingdom is precisely that realm where the will of God is accomplished and the rule of God reigns supreme. As 'heaven' might be defined as the realm where God's will is fulfilled, then the petition is given a tone of urgency, 'on earth as it is in heaven'.

No praying person can listen to the news every day without being acutely aware of the travails of peoples and nations. A brutal act of terrorism claims innocent lives; children die of malnutrition in Africa while the health of children in Western countries is threatened by obesity. HIV/AIDS is a tough call wherever a person lives in the world, but it is still a death sentence in countries too poor to afford proper drug treatments. The news agenda all too often has tragic stories of suffering people which are directly the result of cruelty, injustice and ignorance. These are the issues Jesus confronted in the people he met. It is reported that he touched a leper and healed him when the world wanted only to reject the man as 'unclean'. Jesus gave food to the hungry and with patience taught those who, in their ignorance, were quick to despise the sinner and outcast. The miracles in the gospel story are first and foremost signs of the kingdom of God breaking into this world – healing, feeding, restoring order out of chaos. Listening to the news each day gives urgency to that longing and praying for the kingdom to come: the kingdom, present in the person of Jesus, but yet to be brought to its final fulfilment on earth.

Already it has been noted that Jesus is economical with words. Of course we want to pray for the people who are hungry, the victims of violence, sick people and those who simply survive in their poverty. However, all these things are symptoms of evil, and prayer needs to discern and address the ultimate issue.

Take, for example, the evil famine which has been widespread in countries like Ethiopia and Somalia. A savage civil war consumed vital resources, destroyed crops and impoverished people with little enough of their own. Food given by aid agencies was hijacked before it could be distributed. Fighting between rival gangs prevented medical supplies reaching isolated villages. Clearly what the situation needed, more than food and medical supplies, was a revolution in human affairs that would allow food to get through and medicine to bring healing to the sick and injured.

When Jesus taught his friends to pray for the coming of the kingdom, it was prayer for the confrontation and defeat of a blind wickedness which has allowed such evil to wreak death and destruction. Wherever people are locked in a vicious circle of fear, prejudice and hatred, as once in Bosnia, Northern Ireland or Sri Lanka, then the priority of faith must be for the coming of the kingdom, the overthrowing of evil and the establishment of healing, justice and peace. This is a subversive prayer, undermining all unjust and corrupt systems of oppressive power. It is to pray for the kingdom described by the prophet Isaiah, who longed for one who would come in the name of the Lord:

> The LORD . . . *has sent me to bring good news to the oppressed,*
> *to bind up the broken-hearted,*
> *to proclaim liberty to captives,*
> *and release to the prisoners;*
> *to proclaim the year of the LORD's favour,*
> *and the day of vengeance of our God;*
> *to comfort all who mourn;*
> *. . . to give them a garland instead of ashes,*
> *the oil of gladness instead of mourning,*
> *the mantle of praise instead of a faint spirit.*

(Isaiah 61.1–3)

Such a prayer has to be 'earthed' in the particular realities of the moment but the kingdom is, at the end of the day, to establish mercy, peace and wholeness for all creation.

Bread

There is nothing more 'earthed' than to pray for daily bread.

Give us today our daily bread.

It is a prayer of straightforward simplicity for God to provide our basic need of bread to sustain and nourish us. After all, God provided bread from heaven for his people in the wilderness as they journeyed to the Promised Land.

It is simple enough. Yet for millions on earth, 'bread' is a life or death matter. For them, with barely enough to feed the family today and no guarantee of food tomorrow, life is always a precarious gift. To pray for daily bread on behalf of the hungry people of this world has political and economic implications. As Archbishop Helda Camara once said, 'When I give bread to the hungry they call me a saint. But when I ask why the hungry have no bread they call me a communist.'

In practice, however, the phrase 'daily bread' is one of the most difficult to translate from the Greek of the Christian Gospels. One of the words is very rare and it seems to mean something like this:

> *Give us today the bread of tomorrow.*

In an age which knew nothing of supermarkets and freezers it was clearly important to make provision for tomorrow by having the means to prepare and bake the bread as necessary. It is not just bread for today which is important: if we are to be nourished and thrive, we need bread for tomorrow.

Somewhere in this prayer for daily bread is the idea that God might provide tomorrow's fresh bread – today. It is another way of giving voice to that longing for the kingdom to come on earth, the kingdom which is not yet fulfilled but lies in the promise of God's future. The kingdom where, in the words of Mary's song, the Magnificat, the hungry are filled with good things.

Forgiveness

The kingdom can only be given where it is willingly received. The prayer moves on to confront the barriers which prevent the fulfilment of the kingdom of God.

> *Forgive us our sins*
> *as we forgive those*
> *who sin against us.*

There is a realism here which cannot be avoided. The healing of God's forgiveness is gladly and generously offered, with one provision that such forgiveness will spill over into the healing of every fractured human relationship. You cannot expect to be forgiven if you yourself do not forgive.

Jesus told a serious story of an unmerciful servant who was let off his debts by his master but refused to release his own debtors (Matthew 18.23–35). The story ends with the master summoning his servant:

I forgave you all that debt because you pleaded with me. Should you not have had mercy on your fellow slave, as I had mercy on you?

In Scotland the version of the Lord's Prayer you will hear resonates with this parable, since the words are:

Forgive us our debts as we forgive our debtors.

There is evidence in the teaching of Jesus that divine mercy precedes even the confession of penitence. Jesus goes to the home of Zacchaeus the tax collector before ever Zacchaeus offers to compensate those he has defrauded in collecting their taxes (Luke 19.1–10).

The father of the Prodigal Son rushes out to meet him before ever the lad has a chance to utter a word. There are no preconditions laid down to qualify for God's forgiveness (Luke 15.11). 'You'll get no dinner until you've said sorry,' is the kind of condition some parents lay on their wayward children. It is not so with our heavenly Father. The only condition is that forgiveness should be shown to others in the same gracious and generous spirit. There is a serious purpose in all of this if past wounds are to be healed and cycles of vengeance broken once and for all.

Without forgiveness there is no future.
(Desmond Tutu)

Testing and temptation

The prayer of Jesus comes to a climax in confronting the ultimate conflict with evil:

Lead us not into temptation
but deliver us from evil.

This is a pointed prayer for strength and deliverance when faith is tested, confidence is eroded and evil is confronted. It is the test that Jesus faced in the wilderness when tempted by the devil three times (Luke 4.1–13). The first temptation was to use miraculous powers to turn stone into bread. Jesus was hungry, but this would be to use his powers to meet his own needs. Then Jesus was led up and shown all the kingdoms of the world. If only he would worship the devil and bow down to evil, they could all be his. It is a common temptation to use wicked means to achieve a goal. 'The end', we say, 'justifies the means.' Jesus' answer is to remember that it is written:

*Worship the Lord your God
and serve only him.*

For the final temptation Jesus is taken to the pinnacle of the temple and instructed to throw himself down. Surely this would vindicate his faith. 'If you are the Son of God, the angels will protect you.' Notice the seed of self-doubt which comes with all temptation – '*if you are the Son of God*'. Surely this would make people sit up and listen. They would follow him in droves. But Jesus refuses to coerce people to follow him and, in any case, he is quite clear that to put God to the test in this way is a denial of faith.

So the devil departs 'until an opportune time', and that moment came the night Jesus was arrested. After a last supper with his friends he goes to pray in the Garden of Gethsemane and tells them, 'Pray that you may not come into the time of trial.' This was his moment of decision and his ultimate test. The temptation is clear – flee from the horror to come or even negotiate a way out with the authorities. Both were tempting, but neither was possible if suffering love was to triumph over evil and redeem human nature from all that distorts and corrupts the image of God in the human heart.

This is the terrible moment of crisis for anyone, when the real test comes to deny God, betray Jesus and abandon faith.

'Do not bring us to the time of trial' is another way of expressing the prayer, 'Lead us not into temptation'.

The people around Jesus and certainly the religious leaders of his day would have understood the coming 'time of trial' as the final, cataclysmic conflict in the heavens between the power of God and the forces of evil. Jesus is said to have painted such an apocalyptic picture before his arrest and in preparing his friends for trials and persecutions to come.

> *Jesus answered them, 'Beware that no one leads you astray . . . you will hear of wars and rumours of wars . . . for nation will rise against nation . . . and there will be famines and earthquakes . . . all this is but the beginnings of the birth pangs.'*　　　　(Matthew 24.4–8)

Jewish contemporaries of Jesus believed that out of this conflict would be born a new age, but the birth pangs of this new age would be a time of trial. 'Do not bring us to the time of trial' – do not bring us to that place where faith is tested beyond its limit, and do not abandon us to the forces of chaos in that ultimate battle between good and evil. 'Lead us not into temptation' is a profound prayer from the heart but always remembering that in the Garden of Gethsemane Jesus' own prayer, 'Father, if you are willing, remove this cup from me', is immediately followed by words of absolute trust, 'yet not my will but yours be done'.

From that final plea the prayer moves to a triumphal acclamation:

For the kingdom, the power
and the glory are yours,
now and for ever. Amen.

The psalmist could sing:

Ascribe to the LORD, O families of the peoples,
ascribe to the LORD glory and strength.
(Psalm 96.7)

The prophet Isaiah had a vision of heaven with the Seraphim singing their song of praise:

Holy, holy, holy is the LORD of hosts;
the whole earth is full of his glory.
(Isaiah 6.3)

In the last book of the Bible, the Revelation to John, the song of heaven is taken up by a great multitude, from every nation; from all tribes and people and languages:

Blessing and glory and wisdom
and thanksgiving and honour
and power and might
be to our God for ever and ever!
(Revelation 7.12)

It is fitting, therefore, that in the end, the prayer of Jesus, offered on earth, should be taken up into the music of heaven and echo the angels' songs of praise.

There is one final reason why this acclamation of God's glory follows the heartfelt plea to be delivered from the time of trial.

In the Bible, the story of Job tells of a good man whose faith was tested in losing his family, his possessions, even his health. His wife urged him to curse God and die! But Job, though he argues with his friends and struggles with faith, never curses God. Faith is vindicated when in the darkest times and in desperate circumstances the heart and mind can still offer praise and honour and glory to God.

In the dark hell that was the Nazi concentration camps, one source of light, and one flicker of undefeated humanity, was the regular reciting of the Psalms and the keeping of Jewish holy days.

Rabbi Hugo Gryn, who as a boy was a prisoner in a concentration camp, once told how he had to wind thread to make a wick and conserve their meagre margarine in order that the prisoners might light a candle for their prayers. 'Better to light a candle than just to rail against the darkness.' Even there in that concentration camp, the praise of God was heard from the lips of his children. It is the final and ultimate act of faith and trust.

Questions

1 How do you pray?
2 What do you understand by 'forgiveness'?
3 What in the world challenges your faith?
4 Which part of the Lord's Prayer means the most to you?

The Apostles' Creed

I believe in God, the Father almighty,
creator of heaven and earth.
I believe in Jesus Christ,
his only Son, our Lord,
who was conceived by the Holy Spirit,
born of the Virgin Mary,
suffered under Pontius Pilate,
was crucified, died, and was buried;
he descended to the dead.
On the third day he rose again;
he ascended into heaven,
he is seated at the right hand
of the Father,
and he will come to judge the living and the dead.
I believe in the Holy Spirit,
the holy catholic Church,
the communion of saints,
the forgiveness of sins,
the resurrection of the body,
and the life everlasting. Amen.

Introduction

A 'creed' is a statement of faith and a summary of belief. The word comes from the Latin *credo* – 'I believe'. For many hundreds of years, Christians in Western Europe knew the Apostles' Creed only in Latin, with its opening phrase '*Credo in Deum*' – 'I believe in God'.

The Bible contains many affirmations of faith. The *Shema* (Deuteronomy 6.4) is a fundamental expression of Jewish faith and, indeed, because it speaks of the essential unity of God, it is a basic statement of faith for Christians as well.

Hear, O Israel, the LORD our God, the LORD is one.

'Jesus is Lord' appears to be a very early Christian profession of faith (Romans 10.9; 1 Corinthians 12.3).

And every tongue should confess
that Jesus Christ is Lord,
to the glory of God the Father.
            (Philippians 2.11)

When Jesus, in Matthew's Gospel, asks his followers, 'Who do you say that I am?' it is Simon Peter who replies with a confession of faith:

You are the Messiah, the Son of the living God.

Already in the New Testament, there is a close link between the confession of faith and the rite of baptism, which is the way a person enters the Christian community. In ancient churches the baptismal font is near the door because it is the way in to being a Christian.

As [Philip and the Ethiopian court official] were going along the road,
they came to some water; and the eunuch said, 'Look, here is water! What
is to prevent me from being baptized?' And Philip said, 'If you believe
with all your heart, you may.' And he replied, 'I believe that Jesus Christ
is the Son of God' . . . and Philip baptized him.   *(Acts 8.36–8)*

In addition to these simple professions of faith found in the Bible, there are several summaries of the Christian faith which pre-date the creeds as we have them today but are clearly the seedbed from which the later creeds grew. The 'Rule of Faith' is recorded by Irenaeus, who was Bishop of Lyons in the south of France from about AD 177:

> . . . this faith: in one God, the Father Almighty . . .
> . . . and in one Christ Jesus, the Son of God . . .
> . . . and in the Holy Spirit, who proclaimed through the prophets
> [the plan of salvation].

Hippolytus, who was teaching and writing about the same time as Irenaeus, gives an interesting account of the service of baptism:

> When the person being baptized goes down into the water, he who baptizes him, putting his hand on him, shall say: 'Do you believe in God, the Father Almighty?' And the person being baptized shall say, 'I believe.'

There follow further questions:

> Do you believe in Christ Jesus, the Son of God, who was born of the Virgin Mary . . . ?

and

> Do you believe in the Holy Spirit, in the holy Church, and the resurrection of the body?

The person to be baptized answers each question with the same answer, 'I believe.' Here is the basis of the Apostles' Creed and its threefold structure of faith in one God, who is Father, Son and Holy Spirit.

Both the 'Rule of Faith' as recorded by Irenaeus and the baptism service as recorded by Hippolytus bear a very close relationship to the Apostles' Creed, which is a summary of apostolic teaching, even though it was not written by the first apostles.

Three powerful forces shaped the evolution of the Christian creeds. First was the gospel mandate to bear witness to the faith of Jesus Christ and to 'make disciples of all nations, baptizing them in the name of the Father and of the Son and of the Holy Spirit, and teaching them to obey everything that I have commanded you' (Matthew 28.19–20).

To bear witness to Jesus Christ in a pagan and hostile environment was to risk persecution or even death. To become a Christian in the early Church was a very serious commitment.

> *Do not be ashamed, then, of the testimony about our Lord or of me his*
> *prisoner, but join with me in suffering for the gospel, relying on the power*
> *of God . . .* (2 Timothy 1.8)

Second was the opportunity to teach the faith and give a succinct account of the framework of belief. Baptism, we noted earlier, is the means by which a person becomes a Christian. In the early Church baptism took place at Easter, a vivid and poignant reminder, in dramatic form, that in baptism a person dies to the old life and rises to new life in Christ:

> *Do you not know that all of us who have been baptized into Christ Jesus*
> *were baptized into his death? Therefore we have been buried with him by*
> *baptism into death, so that, just as Christ was raised from the dead by the*
> *glory of the Father, so we too might walk in newness of life.*
> (Romans 6.3)

During the season of Lent, which leads up to Easter, those who had come to faith were given instruction in the Christian way. When they had grasped the essentials of belief, then faith was able to be expressed with a measure of understanding in the form of a creed. This is what you believe both as an individual Christian and as a person who belongs in and to the Christian community of faith. Hence there is the very close link between baptism and the formulation of the Apostles' Creed.

Third was the need to combat error and heresy. The Nicene Creed, for example, drawn up in the fourth century, is at pains to stress the divinity of Christ and came out of the great conflict with Arius of Alexandria, who was teaching that Jesus was less than divine and not of the same 'substance' as the Father.

Behind the Apostles' Creed are all sorts of conflicts and heresies which undoubtedly helped to shape its content. One group of heretics, known as Gnostics, laid claim to a secret knowledge and held that the physical universe is evil and that God did not make it. The first sentence of the Apostles' Creed is not only an affirmation of faith but is also a repudiation of what was considered to be the false beliefs of others:

> *I believe in God, the Father almighty,*
> *creator of heaven and earth.*

Again, there were many fables of gods who died and rose from death, but they were told as symbolic stories representative of, say, new life in spring following the death of winter.

Jesus, by contrast, died at a particular time and place. This is no fable, this is history:

> . . . *suffered under Pontius Pilate,*
> *was crucified, died, and was buried.*

A creed can be very simple, like the one formulated by David Jenkins when he was Bishop of Durham:

> *God is.*
> *God is as he is, in Jesus.*
> *Therefore we have hope.*

A creed can also be quite complex, as in the Athanasian Creed, probably written in the fifth century to combat the heresy that Jesus was not fully human. To wrestle with the Athanasian Creed is to risk a spiritual headache of the first order! It is a useful historical summary of theological reflection but it was not originally designed to be used in liturgical worship.

The Apostles' Creed, because it grew out of the questions and answers found in the service of baptism, has always had an important place in worship as an expression, in historic form, of the faith which binds the Christian community together.

A health warning

A creed is an affirmation of faith. It is no substitute for faith or for wrestling with the big questions faith poses. Nonetheless, a creed is a reminder that others have wrestled with big questions before and left an important legacy in the way that the fundamentals of faith can be expressed. The risk is that a creed, especially one recited as part of worship, can easily become a formula which is meaningless unless some thought and prayer and reflection has gone into trying to understand what faith must have meant to women and men who bore witness to these beliefs in their hearts, on their lips and, at times, costing them their lives in this world.

In all this there is an important paradox. At the heart of Christian spirituality, and indeed the spirituality of other faith communities, is the recognition that the reality called 'God' is the supreme mystery which is essentially unknowable. There is far more to God than anyone can ever know or understand. The *via negativa* – the negative way – asserts that we can only properly claim what God is not and that every claim of what God is carries an element of distortion. The ancient prophets, for example, recognized the limitations of human language in relation to God:

> To whom then will you liken God
> or what likeness compare with him?
> (Isaiah 40.18)

God is not an object in the universe to which words and human notions can properly apply, and it is important to hold on to what the theologian Rudolf Otto called the '*mysterium tremendum*'. This is the sense of awe, dread, silence in the presence of divine holiness. And yet . . . and yet the Christian is called upon to give some account of what is believed by faith, however tentative and hesitant that account proves to be. After all, 'God' is not a word which can be given a clear and unambiguous definition. Saint Paul wrote of the Greek world being populated by 'many gods and many lords' (1 Corinthians 8.6). Even in the contemporary world, the word 'god' is debased coinage, with varying 'cash' values depending on how the word is used and by whom.

The Christian has no use for any confused vocabulary and needs to convey the content of faith as clearly as human language will allow, recognizing that much of what is said will be in the form of symbols and pictures which do no more than point to the ultimate reality before whom we stand and in whom we live and move and have our being.

A creed is like a map of the London Underground system. The map allows you to find your way around the network and delineates the relationship between one line and another, where they connect and where they diverge. It pictures the relationship between stations. The fact that it is a helpful tool in getting about the city suggests that people can trust the truth of what it portrays. However, take the map up into the bright light of day and try to use it to navigate the 'real' world above, and its limitations become obvious.

The Apostles' Creed spells out important relationships in understanding the mystery of God, but it is a limited account which in the end can only point towards the divine reality.

I believe

The Apostles' Creed begins with a statement of affirmation contained in just two words, '*I believe*', but behind those words lie some of the fundamentals of faith. '*I believe*' is first of all a personal statement. At the end of the day I speak for myself. As an adult human being no one can speak for me. No one can buy faith or have it second-hand. For faith to have any reality, you can only bet your own life on it.

'I believe' means laying claim to the truth of God and all the consequences that flow from that claim. Some beliefs do not carry many consequences with them, at least in any practical sense. 'I believe that . . .' is a statement about what I consider to be the truth, as in 'I believe that there is water on Mars.' I have good reason for believing that to be true, but it does not carry any practical consequences for me at the moment.

However, when the statement becomes 'I believe *in* . . .' then it becomes an affirmation of trust. 'I believe in my doctor' says a whole lot more than 'I believe she passed her medical exams.' It is a statement of trust in her as a person which goes even beyond her medical knowledge.

Faith in its practical outworking is about trust, and trust implies commitment. When two people marry and exchange vows they promise to keep faith with each other, and that involves both trust and commitment.

Faith is far more than assenting to a philosophical proposition. Faith – 'I believe in . . .' – is an expression of personal trust and commitment which has implications for the way I view the world, other people and myself. Faith is also the means by which God's transforming grace works within us.

The opposite of faith is not genuine doubt, as that is simply faith struggling to understand. The opposite of faith is fear which paralyses the capacity to trust and breeds a cynicism which corrodes the human spirit. 'I believe in . . .' is the most adventurous statement any human being can make.

God, the Father Almighty

God the Father

Faith, of course, has to have something or someone in which to believe. When the Creed speaks of God, it is not referring to some speculative philosophy but to God revealed in the history of prophets, priests and people, as set down in the Old Testament Scriptures. The God of Abraham, Isaac and Jacob. God revealed supremely in the life, death and resurrection of Jesus Christ. 'The God and Father of our Lord Jesus Christ' (1 Peter 1.3). This is the God in whom Christian people believe.

God the Father is an analogy which must not be pushed too far. God defines the dignity of human fatherhood. The failures of human fathers do not define God! It is to this God that Jesus prayed in absolute trust and confidence – 'Abba, Father'. The God who cares for his children is the origin and source of their being. God goes out to them in love, and as there is something of our human father in all of us, so there is something of God in his children who, in the beginning, were created in his image and likeness.

As Saint Augustine was at pains to point out, the image of God in our humanity has been defaced, though not destroyed, by human sin. In Jesus the image and likeness of God in human expression is seen in all its glory and wonder.

God Almighty

Attention needs to be paid to the description of God as 'Almighty' because it presents a massive dilemma for anyone who believes in the God of goodness and mercy. It has been called 'the problem of evil' and it has proved to be challenging and unavoidable in every age, given the nature of the world and the essential character of the Christian understanding of God. Saint Augustine wrestled with the problem for most of his adult life, and Thomas Aquinas (1225–74) listed it as one of two major intellectual obstacles to Christian faith. In fact it has long exercised the minds of thoughtful people and was even raised in one form by the Greek philosopher Epicurus some three hundred years before the birth of Jesus Christ.

The problem is simply put. In this world we experience the evil of suffering and pain. Yet God is believed to be all good and all powerful. The reality of suffering in the world is inescapable, and therefore if God is all good, God does not have the power to take away suffering and pain. On the other hand, the inescapable reality of pain and suffering could mean that God is all powerful but lacks the will to remove the evil of suffering and therefore cannot be all good. God cannot be both all good and all powerful.

On Boxing Day 2004, news began to come in of a great wave, a tsunami, which had devastated coastal resorts and communities around the Indian Ocean. It took several days before the world learned the extent of the enormous catastrophe that had claimed so many human lives and wreaked such widespread devastation. As the numbers of dead began to rise, and it was understood that the final death toll might never be known, ordinary people seemed to understand instinctively that a huge and costly effort must be made to save the survivors from hunger, thirst, disease and economic ruin. People gave money quickly and generously. Governments, on the other hand, were playing catch-up for several days until, it seems, they realized the depth of compassion felt by their own people.

In the face of such horror, it was as if a 'normal' world view was put on hold and we were seeing life from a different perspective. For a time everything was turned on its head. A long-standing violent feud in Sri Lanka was put on one side as enemies began helping each other as neighbours. In other countries no one thought to ask any cost/benefit questions: the need was too crucial, the time scale too urgent.

Nonetheless, the age-old question was raised, 'Why did this terrible and awesome catastrophe happen?' And more specifically, 'Why did God let it happen?' Let it be clearly understood that such a question needs to be treated with absolute seriousness. Faith is challenged by these things. If it were not so, faith would not be faith as we claim it to be.

To the first form of the question there are several answers, depending on what exactly is being asked. The geophysicist will answer that this tragedy happened because tectonic plates moved beneath the ocean, which so distorted the sea that, literally, a shock wave of enormous power was sent hurtling towards surrounding land masses, destroying everything in its way. The economist might answer that it happened because the surrounding countries claimed they could not afford an early warning system, such as the one in the

Pacific Ocean. The sociologist might want to say that the politicians took a gamble that it might never happen and, as usual, decided that short-term expediency was more useful to them than long-term security for their people. All these answers, and there are others, go some way to explaining why the catastrophe happened and why so many people lost their lives. But there is a deeper moral and spiritual issue in trying to explain why it happened.

In Alan Bennett's play *The History Boys* there is an interesting exchange between a Jewish boy and two teachers. The discussion focuses on how a history question about the Holocaust should be answered. One teacher offers an outline answer explaining why the Holocaust happened. The other teacher is appalled and maintains that such an answer, any answer, denies the moral gravity of deliberate extermination and 'explains' by 'explaining away'. The only proper answer is silence. Faith lies not in any easy answer but in the moral and spiritual need to ask the question. Abraham, Job and even Jesus were all driven to ask in one form or another:

My God, my God, why have you forsaken me?
(Psalm 22.1)

God has set humanity in a regular world of such physical consistency that scientists can understand its workings and can even predict what will happen on the basis of the so-called 'laws of nature'. There are parameters to the physical creation. Planets are formed, continents arise, tectonic plates shift and earthquakes happen. To want it otherwise is to demand a different kind of existence.

The question of faith is not so much, 'Why did this happen?' but rather, 'What must our response be?' In this case it is clear that the human response, the human instinct as an act of faith, has been one of compassion and generosity in order to redeem what is lost and give it meaning in a new future.

This must not be understood in any cheap or trivial way. The most powerful of all the psalms are songs of lament which carry pain, grief, despair and anger. All of this is an essential part of what it is to be human, and all of it is part of our response to great catastrophe and the evil of so much death and destruction.

And yet, strange as it may seem, at the heart of the Christian faith is the belief that in the end evil will not have the last word and that God has the power to turn even evil to his praise.

God judged it better to bring good out of evil
than to suffer no evil to exist.

(Saint Augustine)

And the supreme example is the Paschal mystery of all that is remembered of Jesus' crucifixion on Good Friday and all that is celebrated of resurrection glory on Easter Day.

Having seen how small and vulnerable humanity is in the face of the forces of the universe, might we not also understand how small are the things that divide us? In all our violent conflicts and selfish ambitions, how tragic to add grief to grief. Yet, by contrast, how great is our ability, when faced with unnerving personal disaster, to help the afflicted, heal the injured, comfort the bereaved and give hope to those who have lost livelihoods and homes.

Great minds have thought long and hard, and volumes have been written about the problem of evil. Frankly, it has to be admitted that the malevolence of evil in the world is a profound challenge to faith in the God of love. Evil is so serious that there is danger in giving it a rational explanation as if we could understand it and control it. The first priority is not to explain malevolent evil, let alone explain it away, but to defeat it.

In the Old Testament, the great prose-poem of Job tells how he suffers the vindictive evil of grief and sickness. Throughout the book Job argues with his wife, his friends and with God, until finally God challenges him:

Gird up your loins like a man . . .
Will you even put me in the wrong?
Will you condemn me that you may be justified? . . .
Pour out the overflowings of your anger
and look on all who are proud . . .

(Job 40.6–11)

And Job, finally faced with the inescapable majesty of God, replies:

I know that you can do all things
and that no purpose of yours can be thwarted . . .
I have uttered what I did not understand,
things too wonderful for me, which I did not know . . .
I had heard of you by the hearing of the ear,
but now my eye sees you . . .

(Job 42.2–5)

Job falls silent, but it is not the silence of defeat in the face of evil, rather the silence of awe and wonder in standing before the mystery and holiness of God.

Is it possible, then, to give any sense to the idea of God as 'Almighty'? 'Almighty' is, after all, laying claim to great power. Power is always defined by purpose. For example, an axe is a powerful tool for cutting down trees but less than useful if you try to shave with it. A road drill is an invaluable and powerful instrument when it comes to mending a road but singularly powerless in the hands of a dentist bent on mending the cavity in your tooth.

What is powerful in one context is powerless in another. So if God's purpose is to save the world by transforming humanity in the likeness of Jesus Christ, then suffering love might win the human heart and prove more powerful for that purpose than any amount of military might or social coercion.

In human relationships there is power over people – compulsion – and there is power with people – persuasion.

In passing, it might be noted that the practical struggle of developing democracy in the world has been to replace power over the people by power with the people. It is the only power which ultimately matters.

The different kinds of power are clearly seen when Jesus is brought before Pontius Pilate.

'Do you not know that I have power to crucify you?' asks Pilate. To which Jesus replies, 'You would have no power over me unless it had been given you from above' (John 19.11).

Pilate had the power of compulsion, but when his power was spent in death he became powerless and impotent. By contrast, Jesus refused any kind of power over people but in his own vulnerable humanity had the power to win hearts and minds.

When Jesus meets a blind beggar called Bartimaeus, it is noticeable that he does not even presume to know what Bartimaeus needs. Before anything else he simply asks him, 'What do you want me to do for you?' (Mark 10.51).

It was said that the people were astounded at his teaching because, unlike the scribes, he taught them as one having authority (Mark 1.22). He did not depend on status or position but simply on the authority of truth. And when, on one occasion, Jesus feared that the crowd might take him by force and make him a king, he withdrew to be by himself (John 6.15). He had already turned his back on that kind of power during the days of his testing in the wilderness.

God's purpose is to redeem and transform humanity, and the power of love is utterly consistent with that purpose. When Job said to God, 'I know that no purpose of yours can be thwarted', he was giving voice to his own recognition that God has the power to achieve his purposes and to do so with an integrity and consistency which does not contradict his own nature.

As a boy I used to play in my uncle's allotment during the summer holidays. There was a garden shed which smelt of creosote and contained a wonderful collection of tools, all neatly stored in drawers or hung on the wall. There was an old bath which collected water as it drained off the roof, and there were lollipop sticks used for marking where seeds had been sown. On the slope of the allotment, as it went down to a railway line, I would dig a channel in the ground and build a little dam of earth. Then off to the bath, fill a bucket of water, pour it down the channel and see if the dam would stop the flow. It never did. The water would seem to stop for a while but, sure enough, it would eventually find a way round or under or over the dam blocking the channel. Years later I came across a book written by John Oman called *Grace and Personality*. It is quite a heavy tome but my eye caught a single sentence: 'What all life does say to us is that God does not conduct his rivers, like arrows, to the sea.'

God does not channel his purposes by blasting a way through rock to make a canal. Encountering obstacles of human pride or downright wickedness might appear to deflect God's purpose or even stop it altogether; but in God's good time the river of his purpose will find a way round or under the obstacle and continue its journey to the sea. God's purpose cannot finally be frustrated.

To this end, God is not just naked power. God is love, righteousness, mercy, truth, grace and wisdom. The totality of God's nature self-limits the use of power. God is love and therefore has no power to hate. God is merciful and therefore has no power to be vindictive. God's power is channelled by God's nature. And that is the challenge for us – how to use safely the scientific, technological and economic power that is put into our hands. To handle power safely we have to become something of what God is like, not in boasting arrogance but in concern for the wellbeing of all creation. God almighty: God's power used solely to express God's own nature and to achieve God's purpose.

When finally the human race comes to focus on those important questions of purpose, meaning and values bound up with creating a just and sustainable world, a stable and safer future for all children and a peace that is far more than the absence of violence, then the means to these ends will prove to be suffering love. It is the only power that can do good without the inevitable backlash of revenge.

The foolishness of God is wiser than human wisdom,
and the weakness of God is stronger than human strength.
(1 Corinthians 1.25)

That is the measure of God's transforming grace.

Creator of heaven and earth

The book of Genesis, the first book in the Bible, opens with one of the stories of creation:

In the beginning God created the heavens and the earth.

God did not just make the universe, God *created* out of nothing all that is. Nor did God create the universe and then abandon it to its own devices. God continually creates and sustains all that is. This is what is meant by the Creator God. Nothing in these creation stories conflicts with all that the scientists have discovered about the 'big bang' and the nature of the cosmos. The universe is 'fine-tuned' to sustain the emergence of life and consciousness. Life, conscious of itself, asks the question: why is there anything at all rather than . . . nothing? Consciousness, looking up at the clear night sky and aware of the immensity of the cosmos, feels a strange sense of awe and wonder.

When I look at your heavens . . .
the moon and the stars that you have established;
what are human beings that you are mindful of them?
(Psalm 8.3–4)

'God' could, of course, be a rather infantile projection of the human imagination, desperate not to know itself as a freak accident born out of a cosmic explosion and destined for a cold extinction. In which case there would be little further to be said.

On the other hand, the affirmation that God created and sustains the universe has rarely been used simply as a cosmic comfort blanket. On the contrary, the creation stories in the book of Genesis challenge all human self-perception and raise uncomfortable moral and spiritual questions.

If God created all that is, then life and being must in some sense be sacred, a divine gift. According to the Genesis stories, man is formed from the dust of the earth and God breathes into him the breath of life. There is undeniable truth here. Of dust I am made and to dust I shall return. Eighty per cent water and a handful of chemicals. When it comes to reducing life to the bare essentials, that, as they say, is the bottom line. But that is nowhere near to being an adequate description of the human condition. There has to be room for the creativity of Mozart, the genius of Einstein, the spiritual stature of Francis of Assisi, the moral courage of Wilberforce and the self-giving of countless saints and martyrs. In everyone there is that spark of divine creativity and the freedom to use it for good or evil.

In the Genesis story God plants a garden in Eden – literally a garden of delight – and there the man and his wife are placed to till it and look after it. The Hebrew word translated as 'till' also means 'to serve', and the verb 'to look after' also means 'to preserve'. There is a clear and unmistakable human responsibility in this story to serve the natural world, not ruin it, and to preserve the gift of life, not abuse it. It is precisely the denial of this responsibility which now poses a real threat to the future of this planet.

God made us, not for a pointless existence but to share in the creative purpose of his own self-giving love.

Thou movest us to delight in praising Thee;
for Thou hast formed us for Thyself and our hearts
are restless till they find their rest in Thee.
(Saint Augustine, *Confessions*, Book 1)

Jesus Christ, his only Son, our Lord

I believe in Jesus Christ,
his only Son, our Lord,

who was conceived by the Holy Spirit,
born of the Virgin Mary,
suffered under Pontius Pilate,
was crucified, died, and was buried.

The heart of Christian faith is not a sophisticated, philosophical system but a person with a purpose.

The book of Genesis describes how God placed Adam and Eve in the Garden of Eden, the garden of delight. Yet for most of us life seems to be set in a jungle rather than a garden. On a global scale there are massive inequalities of wealth condemning whole nations to a restricted lifetime of gruelling work and grinding poverty. Perverse and persistent violence, fuelled by fear, spins the wheel of vengeance and retaliation. On a personal level there are all too many times when it seems we cannot do right for doing wrong. As St Paul put it:

> I do not do the good I want, but the evil I do not want
> is what I do.

(Romans 7.19)

Suffice to say that this world is not as God intended. People feel alienated from God, divided among themselves and set on a course which all too often brings destruction and death. Into this maelstrom of evil, chaos and confusion Jesus is born.

From the very earliest days Christians insisted that Jesus was more than just a prophet, more than just a good man, more than just an enlightened spiritual teacher. The human condition might be likened to a person who has fallen down a well, trapped in darkness with no easy way out. Prophets, priests and gurus come along and peer into the darkness, shouting instructions on how to climb the walls and reach the light. Jesus, by contrast, goes down into the darkness to find the lost soul, whom he takes by the hand and brings up and sets free.

Of course, this is only a crude and partial picture of rescue and redemption, but the point is that the early Christians knew that no human being, of themselves, could secure salvation. Only God could save. And yet, unless God entered this world with all our human limitations, then God would forever be shouting instructions through priests and prophets down into a dark well.

The Creed affirms what early Christians were at pains to hold on to in the face of ridicule and torment: namely, that Jesus the Christ was both God and man. They did so in the only vocabulary to hand. Jesus was the unique, the only Son of God, born of a human mother, the Virgin Mary. The point of Mary's virginity is partly to reveal Jesus' birth as the fulfilment of ancient prophecy, 'The Lord himself will give you a sign. Look, the young woman [in Greek, the virgin] is with child and shall bear a son, and shall name him Immanuel [which means God is with us]' (Isaiah 7.14) and partly to insist that this was God's initiative, the fulfilment of God's redemptive purpose.

Born of Mary, conceived by the Holy Spirit. This is the mystery of the incarnation, the expression and embodiment of God in a fully human life.

It has to be admitted that a great deal of complex thought and reflection has been done down the centuries on this central mystery of Christian faith, and many of the spiritual giants of the past would want us to find our own ways in thought and devotion to breathe life into the bare bones of the Creed. Indeed, no proper spiritual understanding is possible without being rooted in prayer and reflection.

> *I give you thanks, Lord, that you have created me*
> *in your image, so that I can remember you,*
> *think about you and love you.*
> *But it is so worn away by sins, so smudged over*
> *by the smoke of sins, that it cannot do what it*
> *was intended to do unless you renew and reform it . . .*
> *Nor do I seek to understand so that I can believe,*
> *but rather I believe so that I can understand.*
>
> (Saint Anselm, *The Proslogion*)

A proper starting point for reflection on the mystery of the incarnation is to ponder those phrases in the Bible which grasp the mind and heart. The truth and love of God engage the human heart first and then invite faith to grow with understanding.

> *And the word became flesh and lived among us, and we have seen his glory, the glory as of a father's only son, full of grace and truth.*
>
> (John 1.14)

> *In Christ, God was reconciling the world to himself.*
>
> (2 Corinthians 5.19)

Jesus prays:

> *I ask not only on behalf of these, but also on behalf of those who will believe in me through the word, that they may all be one. As you, Father, are in me and I am in you, may they also be in us . . .* (John 17.20–1)

Herein lies the paradox of transforming grace through faith. If it is true, as was noted earlier, that in human nature 'the evil I do not want to do, that I do' (Romans 7.19) then it is also true, as Paul recognized, that for the Christian, 'it is Christ who lives in me' (Galatians 2.20) and that any good thing I do is 'not I, but the grace of God that is with me' (1 Corinthians 15.10).

Something of the mystery of the incarnation is glimpsed in the experience of God working in and through human nature at one with the divine will and inspired by the Holy Spirit. Human nature which reserves no pride in itself ('for it is not I, but the grace of God that is with me') is humanity redeemed, restored and reflecting the light of grace and the glory of God.

Lest all this should be deemed mere speculation, the Apostles' Creed then roots the whole thing firmly in history. This Jesus is no figment of the imagination. He suffered under Pontius Pilate, and it is known that Pilate was appointed Procurator of Judea in AD 26. It was under Pilate that Jesus was crucified, died and was buried. In later years there were those who claimed Jesus was not a full human being but only seemed to be like one. They believed he was a divine being, wearing a human body like a coat but not really knowing the triumphs and tragedies of a full human life.

The Apostles' Creed has no time for this kind of speculation. Jesus suffered under Pontius Pilate and died a real death.

God, in Jesus, is despised and rejected, taking on himself the evil of human hatred, hammered home with nails and pressed down with a crown of thorns. God knows the agony of pain and the grief of sorrow for, in himself, God is the Father of a crucified Son.

Where is God in the travails of this world? God is there in the very depths of the darkness.

> *And when human hearts are breaking*
> *under sorrow's iron rod,*
> *then they find that selfsame aching*
> *deep within the heart of God.*

Sin and death and hell shall never
o'er us final triumph gain
God is Love, so Love for ever
o'er the universe must reign.
> (Timothy Rees, 'God is love')

Therefore He who Thee reveals
Hangs, O Father, on that tree
Helpless; and the nails and thorns
Tell of what Thy love must be.

Thou art God, no monarch Thou
Thron'd in easy state to reign;
Thou art God, whose arms of love
Aching, spent, the World sustain.
> (W. H. Vanstone,
> 'A Hymn to Creation')

'He descended to the dead' is a double emphasis on the fact that Jesus really did die. Jesus was fully human even to the point of sharing our death, and in dying joined all those who had died before him.

On the third day he rose again;
he ascended into heaven,
he is seated at the right hand of the Father.

One of the most profound of all prayers is at the beginning of the letter to the Ephesians:

> *I pray that . . . with the eyes of your heart enlightened, you may know what is the hope to which he has called you . . . and what is the immeasurable greatness of his power for us who believe . . . God put this power to work in Christ when he raised him from the dead and seated him at his right hand in the heavenly places.* (Ephesians 1.17–20)

There is no doubt at all that Pilate, the authorities and the crowd shouting in the street all wanted Jesus dead. They put an end to him once and for all by crucifying the life out of him and burying his body in a sealed tomb. And that was that!

Except that history tells a rather different story.

Jesus had been betrayed and most of his friends had run away. In the hours after his death he was nothing more than a memory to a disparate and frightened group of people hiding behind a locked door in an upper room.

And then, against all their expectations, it came to them – or rather, as they could only describe it, he came to them. Jesus was not a dead memory but a living presence, and that is the heart of the event in history called 'the resurrection'.

Easter Day and the empty tomb are important parts of the story, but the heart of it for all the first Christians was the compelling conviction that Christ was alive – and alive in and for them now, not just a distant memory.

It is important to hold on to two important features of the resurrection.

The first is that nowhere does the Bible say that Jesus raised himself. It is always that he *was raised* by the power of God. It is God who, by the power of love, created all that is. It is this same power of love which is also revealed in the life and death and resurrection of Jesus Christ.

Second, the resurrection of Jesus is not to be understood as some kind of reversal of the horrors of Good Friday, a happy ending tagged on to an otherwise appalling death. Jesus appears bearing still the marks of crucifixion. The pain and agony, the betrayal and abandonment are not wiped out but taken up into greater glory. In all the trials and tribulations of this world there was no easy way out for Jesus and there is no easy way out for us. Suffering love is the instrument by which God has wrought our redemption and every Christian is called to share that suffering love with only one promise, that beyond every Good Friday lies the dawn of a new Easter Day.

This is not to encourage some kind of masochistic purposeless misery, but to share in that suffering and personal sacrifice which by its nature is healing, redemptive and life-giving.

> *Rejoice in so far as you share Christ's sufferings, so that you may also be glad and shout for joy when his glory is revealed.* (1 Peter 4.13)

When Jesus is raised from the dead it is most certainly not as a resuscitated corpse but as a new creation:

> *As all die in Adam, so*
> *all will be made alive in Christ.*
>> (1 Corinthians 15.22)

> *Christ has been raised from the dead,*
> *the first fruits of those who have died.*
>> (1 Corinthians 15.20)

So if anyone is in Christ, there is a new creation:
everything old has passed away; see, everything
has become new!

(2 Corinthians 5.17)

It is into this 'new creation' that Christians are baptized, and it is in the life of this 'new creation' that they are called to share.

'He ascended into heaven and is seated at the right hand of the Father.' Of course, this is picture language but with a profound purpose. From henceforth Jesus is a necessary part of the true understanding of God; that is where he belongs. It is a fact that liturgy and worship pioneer the way of understanding. Creeds and doctrines give some coherent shape to what is already enshrined in practice. Long before creeds and councils, Christians were making their prayers through Christ, in the name of Christ and to Christ. That is only possible when it is understood that Jesus and the Father are one. 'Seated at the right hand' is a vivid ancient picture of one who shares the power, dignity and purpose of reigning in sovereign freedom. 'She is my right hand' is another way of saying, 'She is me.'

All this is a portrayal of the truth of suffering love before which every knee will bow 'of things in heaven and things on earth, and things under the earth'.

The empty cross of crucifixion, once a shameful sign of degradation and defeat, stands now as a symbol of triumphant, suffering love over every other force in the universe. Everything that appears to dominate human life is ultimately in Christ's hands, including those mysterious powers which drive us into war nobody wants, stir up economic instability and bring the human race to the brink of self-destruction. Everything is ultimately subject to the sovereignty and rule of Christ. The love of God, triumphant in Jesus, will reign in earth as in heaven, and by that love, seen in the life, death and resurrection of Jesus, are all things finally judged.

He will come to judge the living and the dead

The Creed now turns to the future, but it is always a present future. Anyone who is serious about following Jesus knows that it is by his life that they are judged day by day. Human beings are such insecure creatures. We are constantly comparing ourselves to other people. Paul got so fed up with it that he warned the Christians in Corinth not to set any store by such a practice. The only standard by which to measure human worth is the stature of Jesus of Nazareth.

To look at Jesus is to begin to realize how far short we fall from his humanity. And that failure does not always lie in what we do or think. More often it lies in what we fail to do. Silent, when what is needed is a word of love or forgiveness. Walking by, when a simple act of kind generosity would be life-giving to someone in despair.

This kind of spiritual awareness, judged by Jesus' own life, makes us a lot less ready to condemn someone else. How can I when my own glasshouse is pretty fragile? In all this, and because of the Cross, we believe that God forgives, not easily or with cheap grace, but with costly, crucified love. Being honest with ourselves before God is to be open to that healing, life-giving grace heard on the lips of Jesus in the gospel story, 'Your sins are forgiven you.'

And when finally we stand in judgement before the throne of grace, it will be in the faith and confidence that our judge is one who knows us well and loves us still.

I believe in the Holy Spirit . . .

I believe in the Holy Spirit,
the holy catholic Church,
the communion of saints,
the forgiveness of sins,
the resurrection of the body,
and the life everlasting.

The third section of the Apostles' Creed brings to completion the unique Christian understanding of God. There is one God, and Christians hold to that essential unity, but God incorporates love, intimacy, fellowship, relatedness – community – between the Father, the Son and the Holy Spirit. It is this 'relatedness' which brought forth creation and it is for this 'relatedness' that we are made. No one can be fully human by existing in solitary isolation. After all, it is torture to leave a person in solitary confinement. It is an experience of hell.

Individuals can only be affirmed and celebrated in relation to others. Only in company with others can I truly be myself. Interestingly, it is the contemporary cult of individual*ism* which is the enemy of individuality. 'My view', 'my rights' and 'my needs' are perceived to be what really matters. It is a privatized world which appears to require no reference to anyone else. Autonomous human beings are celebrated at the expense of any sense of corporate humanity.

In the world as it is, however, we are highly dependent on each other. There is but a thread which holds society together. An industrial strike can soon bring things to a stop when refuse is not collected, electricity is cut or fuel is not delivered.

The very being of God, if such language can be used, speaks of a fundamental unity but always in community.

When Jesus no longer appeared to his followers, having 'ascended to heaven', God sent upon them the gift of the Holy Spirit (Acts 2). The Spirit is comforter in the sense of strengthener and inspirer. It is the Spirit of God that Jesus promised to his followers; the Spirit that would remind them of all he had said and done. The Spirit is said to be a pledge, a down payment, on all that God has yet to give us. The Spirit is breath or wind, giving life and power to the people of God. 'Not I but Christ in me' is testimony to the indwelling Spirit of God.

Hence the catholic or universal Church is not just a collection of like-minded religious people but a divine creation, called out from the world as the Body of Christ to the glory of the Father and inspired, given life, by the Holy Spirit.

In that common life the Spirit binds together the great company of saints on earth and in heaven. Christian faith is not a solitary exercise in spiritual enlightenment but fellowship within the Body, in communion with Jesus and all the saints. The transforming grace of God and the harvest of the Spirit are given in company with all who are journeying with us on the pilgrimage of faith.

> *Beloved, we are God's children now; what we will be has not yet been revealed. What we do know is this: when he is revealed, we will be like him, for we will see him as he is.* (1 John 3.2)

The resurrection of the body

Human identity is a complex network of genetic inheritance, upbringing, social context and life experiences. 'Who I am' is the result of where I come from and where I belong. In the Jewish faith belonging to the historic people of Israel is what gives them their identity and provides that important sense of solidarity one with another.

Saint Paul draws on this experience when he describes the Christian community as the Body of Christ. To be a Christian is to be part of that Body. So when Paul talks about the resurrection of the body he has in mind that Christians, by virtue of their baptism, are already one with Christ in his death and one with Christ in his resurrection. It is a present reality and a future hope.

> So if you have been raised with Christ,
> seek the things that are above.
> (Colossians 3.1)

For the Christian, the hope of resurrection is rooted in the resurrection of Jesus and the resurrection of his Body, the community of faith.

There are two Greek words for body: *sarx*, which means flesh, and *soma*, which means something more like the whole person – body, mind, spirit and that network of relationships which make each man and woman a unique person. When Paul talks of the resurrection of the body, he is careful to use *soma*, the resurrection of the person who can only be a unique person in that network of relationships which give us all our identity. From *sarx* we get 'sarcophagus', a stone coffin for dead flesh. From *soma* comes 'psychosomatic', to describe that essential unity of mind and body whereby something real in the mind can have a real effect on the body. Equally, as we know, the physical body can have a real effect on our mental state. That is why believing and belonging go together and why, in the Apostles' Creed, the 'resurrection of the body' stands alongside belief in the holy catholic Church and in solidarity with the 'communion of saints'.

'The life everlasting' is not about life going on in time but rather that eternal life which transcends time and space and which we glimpse in those sublime experiences of love and joy, of beauty and wonder and awe, which even now 'take us out of ourselves'.

> For now we see in a mirror, dimly,
> but then we will see face to face.
> Now I know only in part;
> then I will know fully, even as I have been fully known.
> And now faith, hope and love abide, these three;
> and the greatest of these is love.
> (1 Corinthians 13.12–13)

Questions

1 Complete the following in no more than fifty words:

   I believe in . . .

2 What do you understand by 'Jesus is Lord'?
3 In what way is God 'Almighty'?
4 Which do you find harder – to forgive or to be forgiven?
5 What do you believe about 'everlasting life'?

The Beatitudes

Blessed are the poor in spirit,
for theirs is the kingdom of heaven.

Blessed are those who mourn,
for they will be comforted.

Blessed are the meek,
for they will inherit the earth.

Blessed are those who hunger and thirst for righteousness,
for they will be filled.

Blessed are the merciful,
for they will receive mercy.

Blessed are the pure in heart,
for they will see God.

Blessed are the peacemakers,
for they will be called children of God.

Blessed are those who are persecuted for righteousness' sake,
for theirs is the kingdom of heaven.

Jesus was a teacher. He is pictured teaching in synagogues and even in the Temple precinct in Jerusalem. He is called 'Rabbi', particularly in John's Gospel, and 'Rabbouni', 'my rabbi', is the way in which Mary Magdalene recognizes the risen Jesus in the garden on Easter morning.

Jesus goes up a mountain, sits down and his disciples come to him. It feels as if it is his close friends rather than a large crowd. He starts to teach them what is known as the Sermon on the Mount. It begins with a series of blessings or beatitudes.

Teaching is a skill which demands great integrity. Jesus not only taught by the words and stories he told but also by his actions and by the integrity of his own person. So, for example, he tells the parable of a shepherd who goes out to find a lost sheep as an illustrative story about how God searches for those who are lost. In his own actions Jesus goes out to the sick, to the sinner, to those often believed to be abandoned by God. In himself Jesus is 'the good shepherd' who gives up his life for his sheep. Word and action are one in him.

The bishop who ordained me was a good and holy teacher. After he died it was found that he always carried these verses in his pocket:

Dear Master, in whose life I see
All that I would, but fail to be.
Let Thy clear light for ever shine,
To shame and guide this life of mine.

Though what I dream and what I do
In my weak days are always two,
Help me, oppressed by things undone
O Thou, whose deeds and dreams were one.
                    (John Hunter, 1848–1917)

Integrity in teaching is always the integrity of word and action.

Many of Jesus' stories are concerning the kingdom of God (or, in Matthew particularly, the kingdom of heaven) which is both a present reality and a future hope. More accurately, it is future fulfilment but made present in the person of Jesus. The story of the mustard seed, the smallest of the seeds which grows to become a tree so large that the birds of the air can nest in its branches, is found in the first three Gospels (e.g. Matthew 13.31). Clearly it is a story about small beginnings but also about future greatness. The kingdom of God will be like a tree wherein the birds of the air can build their nests. In the Old Testament a large tree is sometimes the symbol of a great empire, and the birds of the air are the different nations which find shelter and protection under its rule (Ezekiel 31.6; Daniel 4.1). Rabbis sometimes referred to Gentiles as 'the birds of the air'. Here then is a story which looks longingly for the coming fulfilment of that kingdom wherein all the nations of the earth can make their home. It is a vivid story which embraces the earlier vision of Isaiah:

> *Many peoples shall come and say,*
> *'Come, let us go up to the mountain of the* LORD,
> *to the house of the God of Jacob;*
> *that he may teach us his ways*
> *and that we may walk in his paths.*
>
> (Isaiah 2.3)

It is the same vision found in the last book of the Bible where in the end the heavenly Jerusalem is open on all sides:

> *Its gates will never be shut . . . people will bring into it the glory and the honour of the nations.* (Revelation 21.25–6)

But Jesus had already embraced and made present that kingdom of God in and for those people of many different nations he had met. He paid a Roman centurion the highest of compliments:

> *In no one in Israel have I found such faith.*
> (Matthew 8.10)

He heals the daughter of a Syrophoenician woman (Mark 7.26) and elicits the faith of a Samaritan woman (John 4.7).

> *He said to them, 'My mother and my brothers are those who hear the word of God and do it.'* (Luke 8.21)

It is reported that Jesus came to the synagogue in Nazareth, 'as was his custom', and stood up to read the scroll of the prophet Isaiah.

The Spirit of the Lord is upon me,
 because he has anointed me to bring good news to the poor.
He has sent me to proclaim release to the captives
 and recovery of sight to the blind,
to let the oppressed go free, to proclaim the year of the LORD's favour.

(Luke 4.18–19)

In other words, in Jesus the kingdom of God is realized. The miracle stories are examples of that in-breaking of the kingdom. The storm is calmed and the forces of chaos quelled. The blind have their sight restored and the lame are made to stand up and walk. Lepers are cleansed, the sick healed and sins are forgiven. All of them proclaiming the Lord's favour, the rule of God, the kingdom of heaven. Wherever justice is established and mercy is found; wherever there is healing and new life; wherever those oppressed by poverty are set free and wherever sins are forgiven – there is the kingdom of God.

But that kingdom always has a future dimension. It is both 'now' and 'not yet'. The kingdom is here in Jesus but awaits its final fulfilment at the end of time. This future reference is really not about time at all. It is about the 'last things'. It is about what will be of ultimate value at the end of it all. What is seen as important today will probably be regarded as expediency in the long run, and what is prized will probably be of little value when all is taken into account at the end of time.

It is precisely from this 'end' perspective that Jesus' judgements are made. His view of money, in answer to a rich man's quest for eternal life, is 'give it to the poor who need it'. Not because money is of no importance, simply that in the light of eternity it is to be used, not hoarded. Even Caesar (Matthew 22.15–22), to whom taxes are paid, will one day be judged by the values of the kingdom of heaven. In other words, judged by how that money is spent. It is not money which is the source of evil, only the inordinate love of money for its own sake. Money is an important social instrument but it is not, itself, the be-all and end-all of everything.

The 'end of things' is not just about when things come to a stop, like the end of a journey, though it incorporates that as well. Rather, the end of things is about the final fulfilment of God's purpose, triumphant over death and evil. The 'end' of anything is the purpose for which it was made and in which it finds fulfilment. The kingdom of God is always about the fulfilment of God's purpose – and often that purpose is at odds with the way of the world. Look at some of the stories Jesus told.

In the kingdom a wastrel son is welcomed home with open arms. In the world he would probably be met with a closed door. In the kingdom a despised tax collector becomes a generous giver and recovers his humanity. In the kingdom hungry people are fed, not left to forage for food. In the kingdom a Jewish man is beaten by thieves but saved and cared for by a Samaritan traveller. Not so in the world, where the ancient enmity between Samaritan and Jew would have been only too evident.

To even glimpse the kingdom of God means looking at familiar things in a totally different way. That is the power of the stories Jesus told. It means seeing the world, as if for the first time, the way that God sees it.

> *We'll take upon us the mystery of things*
> *As if we were God's spies.*
> (*King Lear*)

The Beatitudes have been called Jesus' 'manifesto' of the kingdom. There is some truth in this but it is very far from being a mere political programme. The Beatitudes signify what the world under judgement will look like and in faith and hope describe something of that kingdom for which all Christians long and pray.

The Beatitudes – background and structure

The Beatitudes are not unique in form and structure. There is some evidence to suggest that there is a background link to the Wisdom literature (Proverbs, some of the Psalms, Ecclesiastes, Job) which also developed in the period between the Old Testament and the New Testament. In fact, there are examples of Wisdom literature in other civilizations. Wisdom literature reflects certain themes, such as the injustices of life, choosing the right way to live, the relative value of riches and the transitory nature of existence. There are many examples of a rather stylized aphoristic form, such as the beginning of Psalm 1:

> *Happy are those*
> *who do not follow the advice of the wicked,*
> *or take the path that sinners tread . . .*

This form is also an example of Hebrew poetry which proceeds not by rhyming words but by rhyming ideas. A good example is found in Proverbs 31.20, where there is no difference between 'poor' and 'needy'.

> She opens her hand to the poor,
> and reaches out her hands to the needy.

Some scholars point out this kind of parallel poetry in the Beatitudes, which would, of course, make them more easily memorable when passed from teacher to disciple. Putting some of them into parallel form reveals an interesting progression of ideas:

Blessed are the merciful	Blessed are the pure in heart
for they will receive mercy.	for they will see God.
Those who are merciful	are pure in heart
those who obtain mercy	shall see God.

Or again, notice the progression of ideas in the banter of these 'beatitudes':

> 'A woman [said to Jesus], 'Blessed is the womb that bore you and the breasts that nursed you.'
> But he said, 'Blessed rather are those who hear the word of God and obey it.'   (Luke 11.27–8)

The Greek word translated as 'blessed' is *makariôs* and can also mean 'happy', but it means more than superficial cheerfulness. Only those who know themselves blessed also know true happiness. By contrast, the world of advertising often uses debased language, emptied of all spiritual content, so that some might even be persuaded that 'happiness is a cigar called Hamlet' or happiness lies in more of everything. In the modern world of virtual living the boundary between reality and fantasy becomes ever more blurred. The Beatitudes call us to a radical reassessment of ultimate truth.

Blessed are the poor in spirit, for theirs is the kingdom of heaven

It has already been noted that Jesus, attending the synagogue at Nazareth, read from the first part of Isaiah, chapter 61, a reading which speaks of God's 'anointed one' (Hebrew *Messiah*, Greek

Christos) bringing good news to the poor and comfort to the broken-hearted.

The Hebrew word translated as 'poor' began by meaning simple poverty. It then developed to mean that because a person had no means of their own, neither did they have any influence, and 'poor' embraced powerlessness and oppression. Finally, it came to mean a person who, having no earthly resources at all, is entirely dependent on God's mercy and grace. Hence one translation could well be 'Happy are those who know their need of God.' It is a parallel thought to the blessedness of the humble and meek.

The risk with all this is that it is perfectly possible to sanitize this beatitude and give it a 'spiritual' value at the expense of a radical realism.

Of course, 'poor in spirit' is a right translation, but it is important to realize there is also a reversal of preconceived values in the kingdom of God. How can anyone consider the poor to be blessed in any meaningful sense at all? Only because in the kingdom of heaven the poor are blessed with help, not blamed for their plight. In the kingdom of heaven the poor are raised up, not kicked down. In the kingdom of heaven the poor are dignified with blessedness, not dehumanized with drudgery.

There are different kinds of poverty, but no amount of sophistry must be allowed to take attention away from those who go hungry to bed, who cannot think beyond tomorrow and die young, worn out by disease and despair.

Then there are those who come up against the way the world is – and lose out. Some are emotionally impoverished, with parents too busy truly to nurture them. Some are intellectually poor because they have no access to education. Some are spiritually destitute because they have nothing more than slogans telling them happiness is more of everything – what Dorothy Soelle once called: 'Death by bread alone'. The Beatitudes, more than anything else, are promise and consolation to those who have no hope and despair of life.

In Jesus' day there were those known as 'the poor in the land'. Simeon, who 'looked forward to the consolation of Israel' and took the child Jesus in his arms when Mary and Joseph came to present him in the Temple, would be numbered among the 'poor in the land'. As would Anna, who never ceased praying in the Temple (Luke

2.25–38). These were devout people who longed for the history of Israel to be fulfilled, people who prayed and fasted for the coming Messiah, knowing that they themselves had nothing and putting themselves entirely into the hands of God. These are the poor in spirit to whom belongs the promise of the kingdom of heaven.

The poor in spirit are those who know they have nothing of themselves, being utterly dependent on the mercy and grace of God. Yet with open hands and hearts and minds they are ready to receive all that God has still to give in the blessings of the kingdom already seen in Jesus Christ.

Blessed are those who mourn, for they will be comforted

Again, how is it that those who mourn can ever be described as 'blessed'? Only because in the kingdom those who mourn are comforted. Unlike in the uncaring world, where those who mourn in Palestine or Iraq or Africa, victims of violence, vendettas, ignorance and HIV/AIDS, are not comforted. They are ignored, dismissed or told they will get over it in time. There is no cruelty like that which is disdainful of another's grief and there is no greater measure of humanity than that we share each other's tears.

Augustine saw in this beatitude that the blessed are those who mourn over their sins and are penitent for their past wrongdoings. There is truth in this but, again, the risk is that in giving the Beatitudes a 'spiritual' interpretation we rob them of their real power.

Living in a world which often appears to harbour a perverse cruelty in human affairs, it can seem impossible to sing the Lord's song in such a strange land where so many lives are lost with such little concern from the wider world. Only when the world truly grieves the genocide in Rwanda and mourns for the innocent victims of war will there be any real resolve for the future. It is just here that humanity must not be allowed to wallow in victim mode by setting aside that supreme capacity for faith, commitment and hope. Faith and hope would simply be a fantasy but for the fact that human beings do grieve for what is lost and mourn for all that could be but is not yet. Strangely, in that mourning is their blessing.

Comfort, O comfort my people
  says your God . . .
'In the wilderness prepare the way of the LORD,
  make straight in the desert a highway for our God.
. . . Then the glory of the LORD *shall be revealed*
  and all people shall see it together,
for the mouth of the LORD *has spoken.'*

(Isaiah 40.1–5)

Blessed are the meek, for they will inherit the earth

'Meek' is a particularly weak word in English. A phrase such as 'meek and mild' suggests a person with no opinions, no will and no character. 'Limp' is the word that comes to mind.

In fact, as you might imagine, the meaning of the word has changed somewhat over the centuries. For the Greek philosophers meekness had about it a certain strength of control. Aristotle once wrote:

> To be angry is easy. But to be angry at the right time, at the right place, at the right purpose, at the right degree and at the right person – that is not easy.

Aristotle defines meekness as the mid point between excessive anger on the one hand and excessive lack of anger on the other. It involves judgement, insight and self-control. It is an expression of humility which does not jump to a destructive anger nor allow an evil to go unchallenged.

The New English Bible translated this beatitude: 'How blest are those of a gentle spirit; they shall have the earth for their possession.'

This is an important insight, for those of a gentle spirit are not without a powerful inner strength. In the world today we can see that those of a gentle spirit are promised to inherit the earth, lest in our human rapacious arrogance and disrespect for this planet there be no earth left to inherit, either for us or, more crucially, for our children and our children's children.

'Might is right' and 'to the victor the spoils' are just two of the many mantras which have been used in the past to justify the exercise of human pride in the violent exploitation of nations and natural resources. But there are other kinds of strength evident in self-control and a different kind of power which is exercised in gentleness.

It is these people who exercise these strengths and power, and only those, who are promised the earth. The alternative is an earth not blessed with life but cursed with a poisonous pollution and laid waste by war.

Blessed are those who hunger and thirst for righteousness, for they will be filled

In the Western world supermarkets overflow with a rich choice of food. Not only is there bread but many different kinds of bread. The capacity to turn a tap for clear, clean water distances us from the vast numbers of people who exist on subsistence foods and have minimal access to water of any kind. These are the people who really know what it is like to hunger and thirst. The longing in this beatitude is the hunger of one who is starving and the thirst of one who drinks or dies.

One of the first credit cards, Access, was launched with the slogan 'Access takes the waiting out of wanting'. Now you can have what you want, no need to wait, you can pay later. Earlier generations who dreaded the loss of control which came from debt and who prized the virtues of thrift and independence would have cast a critical eye on such a claim. But some things you cannot have now. You cannot instantly learn to play the piano. You cannot instantly have the per-fect marriage or the ideal job. You cannot instantly put the world to rights. Any great enterprise takes time, and the perseverance that is needed springs from that sense of wanting, of yearning and longing for what is right.

The one who is blessed is the person who yearns and longs for righteousness, who has a real hunger for justice and goodness. The very desire for it, in spite of past failures and current failings, is the one who is blessed. The Bible has many stories of apparent failure. Moses never entered the Promised Land. David never saw the Temple in Jerusalem. Jesus died a crucified criminal. The important thing is that they never ceased to long for the promises of God to be fulfilled. In that longing God was able to use them in a way that would have proved impossible had they succumbed to some corrosive cynicism and simply given up.

What is at stake here is both the triumph of righteousness in the structures of the world and the personal, individual longing to be right with God. In both senses there is nothing achieved by any partial righteousness. It is all or nothing. Hence the promise is of total fulfilment: 'They will be filled.' Then the wicked will not be seen to prosper and the righteous will be freed from persecution. The imagery is quite consistent with Jesus' teaching. The hungry will be fed from the bread of heaven (John 6.41) and thirst will be satisfied from streams of living water (Revelation 7.17). Such deep longing is a profound expression of faith. It is foolish to want what you know you cannot have. Yearning for the kingdom is, in itself, an intense prayer which comes as a cry from the depths of faith and hope.

Blessed are the merciful, for they will receive mercy

In a world driven by competition, mercy is not viewed as a virtue but as a weakness. Lack of the killer instinct in politics or business is believed to be a prescription for failure. Yet in the kingdom of God this misguided belief is turned on its head. Mercy is not a sign of weakness, because mercy is the prerogative of the strong. Only those with power and authority can truly exercise mercy. In the development of civilizations the judge holding the power of life and death was urged to exercise justice tempered with mercy. Mercy is one of the characteristics of God.

> *I . . . will show mercy on whom I will show mercy.*
> (Exodus 33.19)

Mercy is made possible when the strong are able to identify with the weak and vulnerable. Numerous studies have shown that the most generous people who give willingly to good causes are those who have had a relatively recent experience of poverty, hunger or other misfortune. William Barclay tells the story that Queen Victoria, after the death of her beloved husband Prince Albert, went to visit the widow of the former Principal of the University of St Andrews. When the Queen was announced, Mrs Tulloch struggled to rise from her couch but immediately the Queen stepped forward, saying, 'Please do not rise. I am not coming to you today as your queen to a subject, but as one woman who has lost her husband to another.'

In passing, there is an illuminating feature of the word 'mercy'. In Hebrew the word *hesed* is commonly used, which is a strongly positive word meaning 'gracious kindness'.

> 'The LORD is merciful and gracious, slow to anger and abounding in
> steadfast love. (Psalm 103.8)

But there is another word in Hebrew which is used more sparingly. The word is *rachamim* and the root of this word is *rachem*, which means 'womb'. So the phrase 'Father of mercies' is the anatomically impossible 'Father with a womb'. And yet it sums up exactly the Father who creates and brings new life to birth, the Father who embraces gender in divine creativity.

The love of God cannot be less than the unconditional love of the mother who gives food when her child is hungry, covers her child when cold and comforts her child in pain. It is the earliest love we experience and it is given not because the child is good or deserving or worthy but because this is how mother love expresses itself.

Mercy bestows new opportunity, a fresh start, a new creation. It is ultimately life-giving graciousness to those who have no claim or power of their own.

God in Christ, who knows our human frailties, comes in mercy – in loving kindness. The only condition to that mercy is that mercy should be shown in turn. It is the same principle as that attached to forgiveness in the Lord's Prayer. Only those who forgive can expect to be forgiven. Only those who show mercy can expect mercy to be shown to them.

Blessed are the pure in heart, for they will see God

According to Psalm 24 only those who have clean hands and a pure heart shall 'ascend the hill of the LORD and . . . stand in his holy place'.

Psalm 24 is one of the psalms of ascent, sung by pilgrims making their way to the Temple in the holy city of Jerusalem for the great festivals. What characterizes a pilgrimage is its singleness of purpose in journeying to a sacred shrine or holy place. Of course there are lessons to be learned on the way, and people to meet, but nothing must be allowed to become a distraction from the focus of the journey. John Bunyan's *Pilgrim's Progress* is a classic account of the interior journey of faith. Its full title is *The Pilgrim's Progress from This World to That Which Is to Come*. Christian's journey takes him through such places as the Valley of Humiliation, Doubting Castle and the Valley of the Shadow of Death. On the way he meets the goodly Hopeful and Faithful, the cheating Mr Legality and the evil Giant Despair. The end of the journey is that the pilgrims might 'look their Redeemer in the face with joy'.

It is the same thought that is captured in the letter to the Hebrews.

> *Let us run with perseverance the race that is set before us, looking to Jesus the pioneer and perfecter of our faith . . .* (Hebrews 12.1–2)

Purity of heart comes from that singleness of purpose, dedicated commitment and eyes fixed on Jesus. The person who walks the circus high-wire looks far into the distance, to the end of the wire, and never looks down. At first the journey seems daunting, and frankly it does not get easier with age or experience! But the fact is that Jesus has pioneered the way and asks his friends simply to follow him. Time was when people thought it impossible for a person to run a mile in under four minutes, but after Roger Bannister had run the mile in three minutes 59 seconds on 6 May 1954, others soon poured through the breach. That is what it means to be a pioneer – going where others can follow. The way of Jesus is the pilgrimage of faith, and on that journey it is Jesus who holds us when we stumble and lifts us up when we fall.

> *The greatest glory in living lies not in never failing*
> *but in rising every time we fall.*
> (Nelson Mandela)

Sometimes that fall is long and hard but never so long as to be beyond the reach of his hand. And the journey of faith is undertaken knowing that he has trodden the path before us.

The Greek word for 'pure' is regularly used for corn that has been sifted of all chaff, and this is one of the great biblical pictures of God's judgement.

> *He will gather his wheat into the granary;*
> *but the chaff he will burn with unquenchable fire.*
> (Matthew 3.12)

The Greek word for 'pure' is also used of wine which has not been diluted with water, and metal which has been refined. The pure in heart are those of singular purpose on the pilgrimage of faith and whose motives are unmixed. This is hard, because very seldom do even the most noble of deeds spring from motives that are totally unalloyed. We are fallen creatures in a fallen world. We can only trust that God sees through that mixture of motives and in mercy refines the measure of gold within us.

The pilgrimage of faith is also about learning to see with a clear eye. Princess Margaret and Lord Snowdon used to take their children to the National Gallery, but on each occasion they only went to see a single picture. The temptation on visiting an art gallery is to look at too much and end up by 'seeing' very little. Princess Margaret and Lord Snowdon were teaching their children how to look at a painting, how to attend to it, in order to 'see' it properly. Anyone can walk through a field and look at the various plants, but only those who have learned something of the mysteries of botany can name the plants, describe their characteristics and know their pattern of growth. They not only look but also see the significance of what is before them. The pure in heart are blessed because they shall see God, having learned to recognize his work in the mysteries of creation and his glory in the face of Jesus Christ (2 Corinthians 4.6).

Blessed are the peacemakers, for they will be called children of God

In the kingdom of heaven the peacemakers are given the highest of titles, blessed, in being called 'children of God'.

By contrast, in the world peacemakers can be described as do-gooders, meddling with naive innocence where the survival of the fittest and 'might is right' is the first law of the jungle.

The Hebrew word for peace is *Shalom* and it always carries the sense of peace which comes from justice and wholeness of life. It is never simply the absence of conflict. Peace that is simply factions being kept apart is no peace at all. Peace which depends on dictatorial power suppressing the people is no peace.

> They have treated the wound of my people carelessly,
>   saying, 'Peace, peace',
>   when there is no peace.

(Jeremiah 6.14)

Peace is nothing less than life blessed with that health and wholeness God intended not just for humanity but for all of creation. Such is the interdependence of the whole that no one can fully know the peace of God while there is injustice, suffering and exploitation in the world.

Yet those who want peace at any price simply do not understand the profound nature of *Shalom*.

> *The only thing necessary for evil to flourish*
> *is for good men to do nothing.*
> (Edmund Burke)

The very nature of *Shalom* demands that evil is named and confronted. Passive acceptance of circumstances and situations is not the way to peace. The making of peace is by way of sacrifice and struggle.

To be called 'children of God' is to recognize that peacemaking is the work of God in which the disciple of Jesus is called to share.

There is no ultimate peace without making peace with God, yet it is not us who first make peace with God but God who in Christ has made peace with us.

> *He is our peace . . . he came and proclaimed peace to you who were far off and peace to those who were near; for through him both of us have access in one Spirit to the Father.* (Ephesians 2.14, 17–18)

This is the 'peace of God which passes all understanding'. It is a mystery, not in the sense that it is unknown, but in the sense that it is unfathomable. It is one of the fruits of the Spirit – love, joy, peace – the gift of God to those who are his children.

The work of reconciliation and peacemaking is always open to rejection and mockery, but that too is the way of Jesus.

> *In him all the fullness of God was pleased to dwell, and through him God was pleased to reconcile to himself all things, whether on earth or in heaven, by making peace through the blood of his cross.* (Colossians 1.19–20)

There is energy and purpose in this beatitude. Peace-loving is not enough. Peace-keeping is not sufficient. Only active, purposeful peacemaking is a true sign of the kingdom of God.

As a matter of history, it is the case that, on earth, kingdoms have been built on blood (life) taken. By contrast, the kingdom of God is built on blood (life) given.

Blessed are those who are persecuted for righteousness' sake, for theirs is the kingdom of heaven

The way of Jesus is inescapably the way of the Cross. There have been more Christian martyrs in the twentieth century than in any previous age, women and men who followed Jesus in refusing to compromise with evil or deny their faith. Archbishop Oscar Romero was assassinated in 1980 having spoken out against the military, which waged war against its own people in El Salvador. He wrote to the President of the United States pleading for an end to military aid because 'it is being used to repress my people'. The letter went unheeded. Two months later, the Archbishop was shot.

On the west front of Westminster Abbey there are ten statues commemorating modern martyrs who died in faith, among them Dietrich Bonhoeffer, hanged in a Nazi concentration camp in 1945, and the American civil-rights campaigner Martin Luther King, a fervent believer in non-violent protest who was assassinated in 1968. In this time the Church itself has been persecuted in Uganda, the former Soviet Union and China. Today it is far from easy to be a Christian in Iraq or Pakistan.

In the era of the early Church, a person being baptized and following Jesus put at risk their livelihood, their family relationships, even their own life. At one time the Roman Empire stretched over most of the known world. At first a unifying focus was found in the worship of the goddess Roma. This worship then began to mutate into the worship of the emperor, the one man who personified the empire. At first the authorities tried to discourage it but in the end, as a unifying focus, emperor worship became compulsory. Once a year a man had to burn incense and say 'Caesar is Lord.' He was then given a certificate of loyalty and was free to worship any god he chose as long as it did not cause any civil offence or unrest.

Confronted with the demand to acknowledge Caesar as Lord, many Christians simply refused. For them 'Jesus is Lord' was the only faith they would proclaim, which is why, as an early statement of belief, it was so precious and powerful. Many Christians died claiming that they only had one Lord and to him alone would they bow down and serve.

As the empire could not tolerate what was considered to be disloyalty, then persecution and martyrdom became inevitable.

For everyone who follows Jesus choices have to be made. The Covenant Prayer of the Methodist Church begins: 'I am no longer my own but yours.' That is the fundamental commitment of the Christian to Jesus Christ.

> *Christ has many services to be done; some are easy, others are difficult, some bring honour, others bring reproach; some are suitable to our nat-ural inclinations and material interests, others are contrary to both. In some we may please Christ and please ourselves. In others we cannot please Christ except by denying ourselves. Yet the power to do all these things is given us in Christ who strengthens us . . .*

(Methodist Covenant Service)

No Christian should go looking for persecution; indeed, Saint Paul urges the Christians in Rome, 'If it is possible, so far as it depends on you, live peaceably with all' (Romans 12.18).

On occasion, however, to choose Christ is to invite a persecution that is inevitable. In Britain today there are many ways in which Christians face ridicule from a secular world. It is seen in the press, where the incessant drip of cynicism is a form of mockery. Christians who do not want to work on Sunday find scant protection in law, and refusal to work can cost them their jobs. Work cultures and business practices can sometimes mean that critical choices have to be made.

The real issue in the modern world is actually not far from that faced by those early Christian communities in the Roman Empire. Increasingly, we are seeing the secular state feeling threatened by the public expression of religious commitment. This is particularly the case for the Muslim community, where questions are being asked about where their loyalty truly lies.

It is spilling over into other religious communities as well, where issues of faith seem to be in collision with the laws of the state, or at least with a secular culture. *Behzti*, a play being staged in Birmingham, was taken off after violent protest from members of the Sikh community. Whether that was right in a society which is proud of its claim to defend freedom of speech is open to debate, but there is no doubting the culture clash which brought it about.

Once again we are having to think through questions of loyalty and commitment for those who carry dual citizenship in their country on earth and in the kingdom of heaven.

The Epistle to Diognetus describes Christian life in the second century:

> *Christians do not live in cities of their own or use a different language. They spend their existence on earth, but their citizenship is in heaven. They are dishonoured and their dishonour becomes their glory. They are abused and they bless.*

Those who bless their persecutors, bless and not curse them (Romans 12.14), are walking in the way of Jesus, overcoming evil with good. Theirs is the kingdom of heaven.

Questions

1 In what way do you think you are blessed?
2 Have you ever experienced persecution?
3 Which of the Beatitudes mean most to you and why?
4 How can the Christian community be a peacemaker in the world of today?